Bare Soul

Bare Soul

All illustrations by the Haitian artist Patrick Gaspard.

ISBN: 979-8-9875819-5-7 (hardcover)
         979-8-9875819-4-0 (paperback)
         979-8-9875819-6-4 (ebook)

Printed in the United States of America

Bare Soul

Jean René Bazin PierrePierre

Table of Contents

BOLDLY

DEDICATED

TO

M.G.M.M.

Foreword

Twas just an ordinary day,
Nothing announced what would ensue,
No hint to me made its way through
But there she was, strolling my way.

With no glamour, rather timid,
She looked at this stranger shyly.
I looked at her quite rapidly
But yet my thoughts tempered my speed.

She was different, genuine, austere,
Attired so not to be noticed,
Nothing that could reveal the bliss
That was concealed within her sphere...

But when resigned she went north-bound,
Leaving me dull, in profound pain,
From my heart the tears that yet drain
In these pages their echo found.

True love given from God above
Brands hearts where it chooses harbor.
It never sways in its ardor,
But brightly glows in their alcove.

Tween Us Two

Tween New York and Connecticut,
Tween a job here and a job there,
Tween a smoothie and a doughnut
My mind's curtain suffers a tear
And you appear fresh and uncut.

Tween my short night and my long day,
Tween all the care I so provide,
Tween the times I forget to pray,
I pray mournfully deep inside
For what one day I sent away.

Tween the way home and way to work
Tween the false hopes suffered often,
Tween a thought that my spirit perks
And the rest my spirit dampens
I think of me as a sad jerk.

Tween the wives and the you-know-who's,
Tween the many ones gone too soon,
Tween the ones who remind of you
My heart replays like a cartoon
This love that once was tween us two.

Forever

Now that we've entered forever,
Now that we met at the crossroad,
Now that, at the age of silver,
For life we are blest to reload

On someone to ride the front seat,
On someone to worry about,
To share the joys and the defeats,
The seasons of rain and of drought.

Once again since we have the chance
To hold the taste of what's so dear,
To rekindle our dear romance
Against all the odds and the fears,

We can, since we are empowered,
Safeguard this recovered treasure.
We can, since we have been showered
With blessings beyond our measure.

We will therefore, at light of dawn
Give thanks for what we don't deserve.
And when the moon shines on the lawn
We will pray our love to preserve.

So many times in history
People given this chance once more,
Taking for granted His mercy,
Had lost what they so bargained for.

We paid a price of heavy toll
With long years of sorrow and pain.
We should avoid any dice roll
That'd jeopardize this love again.

So now that you are in my arms,
Now that I can hold you so tight.
Now that I, laden by your charms,
Will get to kiss you through the night,

I solemnly, to the Heavens,
Declare my overdue promise
To be yours until my life ends,
Cherish you till my heartbeats cease.

My Beloved Wife

She wakes up in the morning,
Jovial like a bird singing.
It's always a reflection
Of dreams she doesn't mention.

Then shortly she disappears,
Her voice remains in my ears.
So my cloudy mind pictures,
In the bathroom, her gestures.

She emerges from the steam,
Full of vigor as it seems.
The smile brightening her face
Makes me long for her embrace.

Her frail body maneuvers,
Graciously moves and offers
With the light barely dawning
A spectacle worth watching.

She slowly makes arrangements
And revises all garments.
She knows she is monitored,
She performs to be savored.

The few bites of her first meal,
The make-up she applies still,
All carefully enacted,
All lovingly presented.

Then comes the moment sublime.
I close my eyes for my prime.
Tenderly she comes to me,
Her face closing in slowly,

Kisses me repeatedly,
Makes me promise to only
Think of her all through the day.
Then to work she's on her way.

Then I turn over and pray,
Give thanks for days like today
And thinking of tomorrow,
Hope for the same scenario.

Our Time

There'll be a time for me and you
When love will come back to settle
All accounts so long overdue,
When fears were still kind and gentle.

There'll be a time for me and you
When hand in hand we'll have the choice
To grieve over what we've been through
Or for our gained wisdom rejoice.

There'll be a time for me and you
For then wrapped up in Nature's arms
We will savor what is so true;
The treasures of our inner charms.

There'll be a time for me and you
That will stifle all the false hopes
That crush hearts, bodies and souls too,
Setting a stage for us to mope.

So here's the time for me and you.
Daffodils and lilacs galore
Adorning the stage for us two
To perform love just as before.

Junie, My Angel

Junie my angel
Junie my sweet dove
Come close and dispel
My nightmares of love
Junie my promise
Junie torn apart
Come so I dismiss
All the scars that keep us apart

Junie my angel
Junie peaceful soul
Come out of your shell
Return what you stole
Junie my soulmate
Junie my sweetheart
Come and reinstate
My most treasured part.
Come open the cage
You should have the key
Or break the bondage
It's not that risky
To start a new stage
Where we can write our love story

Junie meek and mild
Junie all alone
Come my blessed child
Come and take your throne
Reign over this land
Parched and desolate
Your time is at hand
Come and change its fate.

Junie fair lady
Junie my godsent
My sole melody
Come give your consent
End this tragedy
My plane long started its descent.

Junie my angel
Junie please be bold
People will come tell
What they know of old
Don't buy any tale
That could make you cold
Their stories are stale
I long paid my toll.

Junie my sunshine
Junie my blue sky
Junie child on mine
Junie sweet and shy,
Be my angel fine
Please, don't let Heaven pass us by

Junie my angel
Junie my refrain
Come write our gospel
And so crush my pain
Open up your mind
Wash your thoughts away
Deep inside you'll find
What the Lord has lay
For our souls to bind
And journey His way

Junie lucky charm
Junie my lifeguard
Open up your arms
Do not disregard
This poor castaway
With gesturing cries
If you go away
He will surely lie down and die.

Us Two

Just by the thought of you
My heart comes genuflex,
Just the mere thought of you,
Right there my mind reflects

On the tender moments
Stolen from your routine,
The wrenching sentiments
That right along they bring.

The sudden summer rain
Can no better surprise,
Nor can over the plain
Any morning sunrise.

Just by the thought of you
My whole world interjects
For brought to life anew
Soul to soul we connect.

One Person

One person in my life it seems,
One person to fulfill my dreams.
One person with a lovely smile,
One person I've known for a while.
One person to make my sun shine,
One person who would claim she's mine.

One person in my arms to dwell,
One person, I know, I can tell.
One person I've been dreaming of,
One person I so long to love.
One person whom my heart beats for,
One person to settle my score.

On person to wrap in my arms,
All dazzled by her childish charms,
One person to say I love you,
One person to pet all life through.
One person I'd give stars and moon,
To one person, my Marijune.

One More Time

To you, and only you, once again, right out loud,
To you, my loving theme, to you, my sweet love song.
Who else, on this green Earth, could open up the shroud,
Where I lie, atoning for all that I've done wrong.

Over my darkest nights, let your guiding light glow
And let your face kindle my hearth when I slumber.
You alone hold my hand in my everyday flow,
Bringing me heaven's treats in impressive number.

Subtly, day after day, you bestow your goodness,
Hovering on my soul, ensuring my safeguard.
When you barge on my mind, I perceive your finesse
Which gives me strength to stand what comes to my regard.

Aren't you in demand to a much worthy bunch?
Aren't you here, spoiling a non-deserving soul?
Precious jewel of my case, my most spirited punch,
You reveal to my soul the God I should extol.

When you set your brown eyes on my world small and bleak
And gently come and brush my wrought-up attention,
The thrill deep within me brings me up to the peak,
Where I can hear angels in blissful rendition.

When with your tender touch you came soothe all my ills
I knew then, for certain, I'd found my pot of gold
And like the wise brethren who discerned a good deal,
To safeguard it, quickly, all that I had, I sold.

And I even worship the ground you tread upon,
Like the sweetest Mama, well-endowed of wisdom,
Like a gentle sibling always there to lean on,
Like the only daughter you thought would never come.

Alas! I love you so that the sound of your name
Bring tears into my eyes and a knot in my throat.
And in this icy land, my heart and soul you tamed,
Pine all day and all night. So, this to you I wrote…

O Lord, make that one day, one of these autumn eves,
Guided by Your Spirit, she makes her way to me.
Until this blessed day, with heart set on my sleeve,
I will pray that her eyes will never be gloomy.

Your Love Song

I will never believe
That others won't receive
None of this legacy
Framed by this secrecy
Of the so many views
Of the bond of us two.
If I should die today
Despite the come what may
I hope my dream come true
To write you a love song.

For you, my darling dear
I wish I could draw near
The perfect choice of words.
So many ones are stirred
Cascading endlessly
Over my mind's valley.
I tried to make them mine
But I could never find
The right set finally
To write you a love song.

So many the dramas
And pay back of karma
We had to see right through.
Some for me, some for you
But always to enhance
Our wicked romance,
Joining you, joining me
Today we patiently
Pray that our dream come true
And make you a love song.

But to nourish the flame
In vain I tried to tame
This semantic downpour.
I shout like none before
But the crowd on my path
Though they try not to laugh
Will always veer to me
When they hear that I spree
The love I have for you
And write you a love song.

Without You

From the depths of my lonely soul
I long for you to make me whole.
The thoughts of you that linger on
Give me rainbows to glide upon.
I dip my mind ov'and over
In the souvenirs you offer.

But all the while my empty stare
Docks the shore of an isle so fair;
Your lovely face, which tries to hide,
With a smile where my fate abides,
The promise of a me-and-you,
The certainty of love brand new.

Unceasingly your realm of love
Draws in my soul so deprived of
Its mere essence of survival.
There, longing for your arrival
I dream of golden tomorrows
That'd make amend for my sorrow.

Through mountains high and valleys low
I will seek you my sweet sparrow.
We will rekindle the blessing
That by your absence is stifling,
Making my dreams of future bliss
A happy scene hard to dismiss.

From the depths of my weary soul
I beg of you, come take control
Of this ship drifting aimlessly,
Of this heart racing painfully.
For in this dark and icy land
I yearn for the warmth of your hand.

Insight

In flowery meadows of my mind,
You pace lightly, pace silkily,
The flowery meadows that I find
When thoughts of you come down swiftly.

In the spring valley of my heart
You run solely, so steadily,
The spring valley that would infarct
If far from me you would journey.

But in the kingdom of my soul
Your name shine on every banner.
Against all odds we will grow old
With blessed peace as a treasure.

Your Eyes #1

Every blessing the Lord bestows
Declares out loud His love for us,
Through the joys and through the sorrows
With His Spirit deep within us.

More then often in His wisdom
He goes surpassing His mercies
And so the blesséd outcome
Lingering unbelief, unfreeze'

Nothing on Earth says it louder,
Nothing His blesséd love can size,
Nothing can attest it better
Than the look I see in your eyes.

Sun And Moon

The moon said to the sun
I'll catch you, I'll catch you.
So tirelessly she spun
After the dazzling hue.

The sun steadily sprang
In the sky faded blue
And in galactic slang
Replied I love you too.

And the earth all-tipsy
By the relentless chase
Wishes never to see
The ending of this race.

The sky would never bless
This all forbidden love
For when one is at rest
The other shines above…

Pray to the Creator
Our love to attune
For without His favor
We'll be like sun and moon.

In The Quiescence Of The Night

In the realm of my audition
I feed on the deafening silence.
Not a bug is given a chance
On this, my side of horizon.

What times carries this cloudy sky
Who sneakily muffles the stars
But spreads from some beacon afar
That shade of brightness way up high?

Closer to me a soul shivers,
Into my arms a body trenches
But it's in vain my thirst she quenches
So much is the horn she triggers.

Stay close to me, the day is done,
I want to pull you in my dream
But let me first ignite your scream,
Break the quiescence of the night.

The Girl I Love

One of these mornings I woke up,
Tired, weary and all fed up
Of the continual happenings
That trouble us, all living things.

So I nonchalantly got up,
Looking for what could cheer me up.
Gently on my thinker, sweet dove,
Gently came perch the girl I love.

She's no goddess, no cover girl
But nonetheless makes my heart swirl.
She' s no Marylyn, no angel
But my mixed feelings, unravels.

She brings to me the light of day.
Her face I see each time I pray.
Whether sent by Zeus, God or Jove,
I still treasure the girl I love.

So through my life I go daily,
Some happily, some painfully
But deep in her brown eyes gazing,
I feel I can do anything.

Blessed Perseverance

The traveler lounges under the still shadow,
In the midst of this vale, all alone, he daydreams:
Here a cheerful bird chase, here a dancing willow
And the brook shouting muffled screams.

But nature with its laws, in many instances
Brings to a gentle soul its share of grave burden.
Of a narrow escape, what are the fat chances,
That he dies early in its den.

Here sitting in this vale, he longs for such a break,
Traveling yet so far, lacking yet what it'd take
To dismantle his miseries.
And down his weary sight, only looms the faint hope,
Through all the passive clouds of his arising slope,
With his tomorrow's mysteries.

Gloomy and dejected, on the road straight ahead,
Nothing, of his fancy, can tickle the meek shed.
He craves a kindred soul for this dreary journey
But in vain, for alas, on this rotating sphere,
No one will come efface the look bleak and austere
That chases away so many.

He long gave up the fight, and the look of his stance
Favors the dark cypress, never given a chance,
In this forlorn valley. It stands tall and erect
And never has it been, to lighten its figure,
And revamp its gloomy tenure,
That a devoted vine, its trunk would come prospect.

So before he resumes his long, dreary travel,
After a short respite and mental escapade,
The lonely traveler, leaving the soothing shade,
Drags the hefty silence, helpless to unravel
His solitude that would not fade.

Trees, ponds, growing bushes, from one another stray,
Yet so serene in all your ways,
Come all and lend a hand to this young fellow's plight!
Gentle brooks; come awash, with your cool flowing streams,
His ever-weary feet from the mire and the themes
Of the City's numerous sights,

Under your soothing shades, grant that he comes recline,
And in sweet somnolence, his state of being, refines!
And the lovely maiden, queen of his mind caper,
Who comes in every time to offer sweet solace,
With her angelic voice and in tender embrace,
His gloomy heartache, she'll taper.

Nothing can bind his soul, soaring high to its bliss,
To fall in unison with treasured souvenirs.
Nothing else in this life can preclude him to miss
What he once knew and what, day after day, he nears.

When will I see your face? Tell me, when will you bless,
O star with warmth aglow, O beacon of my night,
With your sweet soul, my den meekness,
To cast away this dull and dreary sadness plight?

He'll never reach the shore of this isle of his dreams
Despite the deep longing of his soul in distress.
But rather he relies, as foolish as it seems,
On the goodness of He who hears the silent screams
Of those yearning for a mistress.

But O goodness! Behold! There she comes from afar!
Farewell to you, cradling streamlets!
Farewell I bid to you, sweetest vale that you are,
Farewell bosket, venting outlet!

Blessed be the lonely who, with nature surround,
His soul deepest illness, he can just ventilate.
Since his relief cannot be found
He trusts Heavens for his clean slate.

Waiting For You

In the darkness of my bedroom,
I see shadows and taste my gloom.
I see forms fade with my blank eyes
But in my mind I see bright skies.

My heart fibers bleeding for you,
The thoughts of you, always brand new,
Dictate my mind, ignite my soul,
Rush through my body as a whole.

I think of time when we were us,
Time so little, time so precious,
Time when we showed the way we cared
But that destroy the love we shared.

I think of things that could have been
Then I promise in life foreseen
To love you more each day I breathe.
And when you're joined with me that eve
I'll kiss you at every sunrise.
Our love then will be concretised;
You'll have my name; I'll have my queen.

Lost Soul

In the dark alleys of my night
I call your name with voice of fright.
As though to save my frantic soul
I search and search for you to hold.

The dreadful feeling nursing me
Reaps from my soul pure misery.
It pronounces the verdict cold
That right before my eyes unfolds;

The days to come will bring to me
Painful burden of infamy
But in the depth of my cold night
I miss the warm glow of your sight.

Painfully it dawns in my mind
That you willfully left behind
This vengeful curse to abrade me,
Me and my loathed polygamy.

For when you came in to my life
You chased away my inner strife,
Brought me your smile, brought me your love
And the blue sky from God above.

So I relentlessly pursue
This trail of love, this shade of blue
But mercilessly I come back
Time and again on my first track.

There, in this terrifying maze,
Deprived of the least of sunrays,
The stampede felt within my chest
Favors a derby at its best.

So many times your sunlight rose
Upon my mind which long time froze,
Your lovely bouquet, which lingers
To underline all my errors.

And the free fall that never ends
While I desperately seek your hands,
Proclaims aloud from land to sea
That your brown eyes I'll never see.

And suddenly I come to grip
That what I sow is what I reap
And though for you I now hunger
I'll enjoy your sweet smile never.

Oh I lost your silky shadow
In this maze of columns and rows,
I lost my heart that followed you,
"See", you would say, " Didn't I tell you?"

But I cling to my emptiness
Of love, blue sky and your caress
For this whole world of nothingness
For ever seals my cursedness…

So if you see through your window
A lonely wandering shadow
That seems not to know where to go
Don't you go laugh at its sorrow.

For the dark alleys of my night,
Where I holler with voice of fright
Portray my soul resting in shroud
While still calling your name out loud.

Alone

And so alone I stand,
Alone, with empty hand,
Alone without a dream
Thinking it's just a scheme
The silent one in me
Feeds me repeatedly.

Alone, no one to vent,
Fearing I may repent
From seeing their faces,
Or hearing faint traces
Or worries they'd harbor
When faced with my candor.

Alone, facing my fears,
Alone, wiping my tears,
When unannounced you come
And make my mind your home.
Alone, my heart in trance
Begging for one more chance.

Alone, oh so alone
But polishing the throne
That my heart, though captive
Has lovingly conceived
For you I so adore,
You, I yearn and pine for.

And so alone I'll stay,
In silence beg and pray
For the twin of my soul
To come and pay the toll
To this love tearing me
And at least set me free.

Last Chance

Be my solace,
Bring to my face
The grin so foreign yet so dear.
Be my solace
Come and erase
Of my drawing all shades of fear.

Far away from the life we live
We often ignore the missives
Sent to us with design to break
The loads of strives we keep at stake.

Far away from your smile I miss
My ever-needed inner peace
That drifts aimlessly on this raft
Heading for Niagara's path.

Be my fraulein,
Come rain or shine
Into my life of empty rooms.
Be my sunshine
Come redesign
The landscape of my lifeless gloom.

Life's not meant to be lived alone,
Love is the gift of one's person
The lonesome ones who don't bother
Miss Heaven over and over.

So come give me my share of grace,
Of my stigmas don't leave a trace.
This life is given, not our own.
For all my flaws let me atone.

Honey Moon Song

O come my lovely child,
Come rest yourself by me.
See how the night is mild
And the stars are many.

They're here to celebrate
And bless our first embrace.
They shine as to relate
To us their borrowed grace.

Always they'll remind us,
If ever we forget,
In case we are devious,
Of the time we first met.

So the vows that we swore
To us before the Lord,
More than ever before
Should seal our accord.

For the world is ready
To smother in our hearts
By words full of envy
What flame made us sweet-hearts.

Come, come my blessed child,
Restore yourself in me.
Soon the moon will have miled
And the stars will all flee.

When The Sun Takes A Bow

When the sun takes a bow, shunning the paysage,
Shying from rusty skies in a golden moment,
Tenderly I hold you, the source of my torment,
Star of my quiescence and my inner rampage,
And we remain embraced, free of any comment.

Nothing troubles the squeeze of meeting you anew.
It remains undisturbed as the glow in your eyes
That mirrors the pleasure of idling in these ties,
Tailor made by the love binding us, me to you,
Fleeting as you can be, though bearer of dusk prize.

At this very set time come perform on my scene.
Nothing's hidden from you, how deep within my mind
Where the seasons remain ever loving and kind
While the stampede in me, half scary, half obscene,
Robes me with ecstasy, while I'm half lame, half blind.

Though you never linger, drifting in your essence,
You permeate my mind in a nick of a glance
Long enough to ignite this perpetual romance
Cause of the stifling breath branded by your absence;
Always with just one look you blot any offense.

Come Home

Come home to me,
Let's end this misery.
Come home to me
Let's work at being happy.

The days drag without you into senseless evenings
And even old Trixie will not lick its pudding,
The flowers faded away
And the grass has turned to gray
And the squirrel gave up its early day begging.

Come home to me
I never meant to say,
Come home to me
The words you heard that day

They were only mere thoughts of a deep troubled mind
Expressing the sorrow of a past left behind.
To who's bitten and twice shy,
All is first seen as a lie
And just disconcerting when honesty he finds.

Come home to me,
Come bring life to my world
And you will see
The way I treat a pearl

For the bedroom mirror misses your reflection.
It looks much lovelier bringing your description,
Either your eyes of pure jade,
Your many dancing parades
Or your modeling spree done with verbal caption.

Come home to me
Come and get back your baby,
Come home to me,
Let us work at being three.

Once I Had

Once I had her and the sky
And all the stars shining so bright
Once I had her tenderness
When in my arms I held her tight
Once I had her soft kisses
Showing me Heaven in plain sight
Once I had a steady love
Daily helping me in my plight

Once I had her hand in mine
Leading me out of any fight
Once I had and now I know
You don't own your tomorrow.

Once I had her and all I did
Was play around like a child
Once I had her and it seemed
She tried so hard not to chide
Once I had her and often
I tried to make her my bride
Once I had her and she knew
The so many times I lied
Once I had her and at times
I was led on by my pride
Once I had her and now I know
I alone nursed my sorrow.

Now I have between my arms
The never-ending thin air
Now I have between my arms
What everyone thinks is fair.
Once I held her in my arms
And all burdens I could bear
Now I have as a reward
My heart her absence just tears
Now I have and to the world
My love for her I declare
Once I had but now I know
You reap whatever you sow.

Farewell

I will go on my lonesome way,
No more I love you will I say.
Since the string of love you sever,
There will be no more us, ever.

Repeatedly, time and again
You made it very, very plain,
That me, myself and all my love,
You wanted none of the above.

Once you uproot yourself, you said,
Made up your mind three years this may,
Nothing on earth would make you change,
Not ever your life rearrange.

So now the love table has turned;
To have your hand, I long and yearn,
Begging of you to please accept
The plea of love that I excerpt.

The knells of life did once again
Ring out to make me understand
That what you may find in the night
You lose sometimes in broad daylight.

To Pray, To Love

I always wonder
Every time I pray,
Why my heart jitters,
Drifting down your way.

Every time I yearn
For my dear Savior,
Slowly I discern
You in my mirror.

As He once taught me
If I come to Him
I would learn slowly
To love without scheme.

Barclay Avenue

Caught in the stillness of my night
I see your face.
And since my thoughts so far are bright
I found erased
All the worries of my today;
They magically just fade away.

It's always the same scenario.
First you appear then the ratio
That you generate with the zeal
Caused by you fondling my heart still.

You are my light in darkest days,
You are the bright sun of my rays,
You are the soul I'll be searching
Long, long, after my life ending.

So don't ask that I should forget
What we once had.
I still love my darling "Hornet",
Color me mad…
You magically just fade away
All my worries of any day.

M.G.M.M.

O come my lovely one,
Come and see how undone
This heart you once forsook
Remains without the brook
Of love and tenderness
That you are, my princess.

O come my beloved,
See how perfectly made
The bed of scented rose
With the finest of clothes,
All picked at your measure,
Your soul to recapture,

O come my angel fine,
Come again and be mine.
Long, long, so long ago
My heart to yours echoed.
Come therefore, please return,
His love plea, do not spurn.

Love

Love should be given hopelessly,
In return expecting nothing.
May what you spread generously
Not come back to you shortchanging!

The love you sow along your path
Blesses your divine counterparts.
In return the Giver of life
Grants the desires of your heart.

Foolish is the one who believes
That he should pamper himself first.
By serving others one retrieves
Graces galore that one can trust.

For the connection that we share,
Precious and divine in aspects,
Makes that minding others' welfare
Brings back a positive effect.

But this should not be the reason
We care for the needy brethren;
Love resides in every person
Then should be cherish and sustained.

I love you therefore hopelessly,
I love you with my heart and soul.
Cherish you I will do daily
Until we are a blessed whole.

Caspar

The Pillow

This pillow that I hug so tight
Recalls your scent of our last night.
My lonely heart skipping a beat
Misses sadly its lovely treat
And this nightmare of your absence
Comes back to me as cruel nuisance.

Then quietly my mind evades
To a land of much lovely shades,
That dreamland where you reign as queen
Where I can bathe in sweeter scenes…
And the pillow watching the show,
Applauds when hand in hand we go.

Birthday Wishes

Why are people driven towards one another,
Remains a mystery.
But whether to stifle the feel or to utter
Can be a misery.

To confide or not to
My sweet tickle for you
Is the plight I carry
While wishing you're happy!

Lost Love

But I'll go miles, way down the years
Longing for you, hiding my tears,
Chewing upon the happy days;
Just sentence my bleeding heart pays.

Never you'll know; life's so unkind,
How much you remain on my mind.
But in the mean, non-ending while,
I miss your loving, childish smile.

But if ever – God is so good –
You drop by in my neighborhood
And if again from up above
Love swoops down on you like a dove

Then I'll go miles, way down the years
Upon my face showing my cheers,
Inventing lots of lovely ways
To keep you in my arms always.

The Words I Say

It's always what I say; it's never what I write.
I see you so clearly, like the moon late at night,
Like the Bethlehem star on my lengthy journey,
You surely lead my heart to you, my sweet Junie.

It's always what I say though sometimes I recite:
"I can't fall out of love though she's so out of sight".
Just like the sure anchor of this boat in distress
Carefully I hang on to you, my sole mistress.

It's always what I say, fearing to feel the fright
Of rising tomorrow in darkness or in light.
The dusk that would befall if I never see you
Or the dawn I'll enjoy the day my dream comes true.

It's always what I say; say you will, say you might
Turn back the hands of time, come back and hold me tight.
And like nature's rebirth at the dawning of spring,
Over my cold season return and do your thing.

She And I, Both

Riding this uptown train, we, on the way to work
Met one day, eye to eye. She, so proud, I, the jerk.
Thoughts ablaze, eyes on fire, in silence we exchanged
Muffled inquiries of each other's status
Our eyes at each other's necks held on mordicus
But this to us never seemed strange.

Just like two birds lost in a crowd of city fair
We dangled up and down holding each other's stare
Sustaining the queries, stifling every reply
That could under this light reveal the silent screams.
Deep in each other eyes we could perceive our dreams
But on faith we could not rely.

So we went through the stops but no passenger dared,
By blocking our view, perturb this love affair.
It seemed as the first time that we had us noticed ,
It seemed as the first time, but despite empty seats,
Nothing had permitted this lovely duel to quit.
Face to face we chose to insist.

No verbal cue offered, no touch, no wink, no sign,
Nothing ever revealed that one day she'd be mine.
And I would verify that though loud in her thoughts
She had quickly dispelled this clear story foretold.
She never imagined, race barriers put on hold,
We were the true love we both sought.

A Man

A man
Once had a dove
Just plain
But full of love.
He thought
In righteousness
Let's not
Live in a mess.
So he
Opened the door.
Slowly
What he lived for
Freely
Took her first flight
Sadly
Left him in plight.

Took time
For him to assess;
His prime
Was queen of his chess.
Alone
With his emptiness
In prone
His face in distress
He prayed
For the Lord's goodness.
He lay
Waiting to be bless'.
Maybe
He thought to himself
Will she
My sweet little elf
Return
To her lovely nest
Not spurn
But revive my zest.

Junie,
O my sweet queen of heart,
Chérie,
You have torn it apart,
Truly
The day you did depart
You are
The sole cause of my joy,
You are
The grace He once deploy',
You are
My true essence of life,
By far
My other, better half.

Silent Words

Should I tell you how much I love you?
How you have made my dream come true?
The silent words I don't utter
Deep inside of me I mutter.

You should not hear the strong racing,
You should not see the blank staring,
You should ignore that through my day
Nothing, nothing comes in your way.

You take over at early dawn
And often comes to trip my yawn
For the smile surging within me
Carries your stamp, O my baby.

So there, these words I don't utter
Always come causing my laughter.
Along with you, my dream came true,
So why should I say I love you?

Cherry Love

Close to me so loving
Glide into my arms
With your shadow dancing
Touch me with your charm
For my Cherry Love,
Time is a big tease
For you my betrothed
And the birds and bees.

From the look of all
It doesn't make sense
Listen to my call
Give our love a chance
Open up your pod
Say you love me too
For the love of God
Please let me go through.

Now down on my knees
I long to savor
O my darling please
Let me devour.
You can moan and groan
You can call all saints
But there, on your throne.
Give me your consent.

Right against the norms
And all the taboos
Let your brook perform
Pouring your sap through,
I drink your substance
Like a fish stifling
As a recompense
You give my thing.

And the moon connives
With mounts and valleys,
My pen's inner drives
Merge into follies.
Like shivering pups
Under southern skies
The night's envelop
Gives us wings to fly.

Close to me, still loving
Glide into my arms
Now shadow whispering
Touch me with your charm
For my Cherry Love
Time is a big tease
From Heaven above
For all birds and bees.

Bitterings

I told myself so many times before
To shut the door and wait for nothing more.
I had my chance but in my ignorance
I senselessly refused her the last dance.

So now it seems I became a bit wise
This heavy fog's been lifted from my eyes.
I see clearly just what she meant to me
And without her just what my life will be.

I begged out loud the good Lord I treasure,
In His mercy, to restore my measure.
I cried out loud facing my loneliness,
Always tasting of her hands the caress.

Day after day I carry this burden.
Within my ears the voice of her, remains.
Within my heart, her love that I long for
Depicts my life in senseless metaphors.

I go through life so full of lovely shades
Of emotions as in joyful parades
But within me one color always stays;
A taunting gloom turning my world to gray.

And so it is that I long for her hand
Though many tears ever between us stand.
I'd give my life for a glimpse at her face,
I'd give the world to my mistake erase.

You hear stories of dead-end love affairs
But you never fathom the hearts they tear,
The many lives that slowly they stifle,
Even the souls that they leave all baffled.

The lowest point of my life will remain
That sad instant she walked into that train.
I stood there still sizing the anarchy
That rapidly swan dove right within me.

And ever since that heart-wrenching hour
I taste my life so bitter and sour.
My inner drive she took to who knows where
Leaving me pain and impending despair,

I will treasure every mem'ry of her
And call her name in my dreams whenever.
She will always reign on this lonely heart
Though in her flight she took its major part.

I beg of you please, go remind my son
That what you do you fail to get back none.
Unselfish love and faithful devotion
Are of this life the joyful solution.

Then I remind myself as an encore
To shut the door and wait for nothing more.
Though chances are, despite my ignorance
One blessed day I will find deliverance.

The Taste Of Things That Passed

The bitter sweet,
The all cherished,
The painful treats,
The unfinished,
Each time they ring
Deep in your ears
They always bring
Unpleasant tears…

Will you ever forget this love,
Will you finally get rid of
This kneeling feeling that her name
Imposes on your heart she tamed…?

The lonely beat,
Impoverished,
Who did not meet
His so cherished
Dances with slings
Of lonesome fears
To the beguine
Of you, my dear.

And I Think Of You

As I wake you, I think of you
What time it is, I think of you
I got to work today, I think of you.
And as I pray, I think of you
Got to shower, I think of you
I'm running late today, I think of you.

You never seem to leave my mind,
The thoughts of you bind
Every ounce of my being since I met you
And happily I go my way
To hear people say:
He seems to have been touched by some one brand new…
So brand new.

And as I work, I think of you
I meet pinays, I think of you
My patients call my name, I think of you.
I sit to chart, I think of you
It's time to snack, I think of you
Oh I am so sleepy, I think of you.

Suddenly I seem to exist
Now I can resist
To loads of stress I could not suffer before.
For my life's taken a new twist;
It's heavenly bliss
Where I seem to get from you kisses galore…
And encore.

When I drive home, I think of you
It's gonna rain, I think of you
What a traffic tonight, I think of you
And when you come to me,
In my arms my baby,
I'll shower you with what the thoughts I held to myself, carry.

To My Baby

O my lovely,
O my Baby,
You true cause of my lunacy,
You have my nights topsy-turvy,
My days, your name's a litany.

Time after time I see your face
That's when my heart runs a fierce race
Where every beat seems to reveal
The love I carry for you still.

And all the while,
In my exile,
Though between us are many miles,
Your voice of dreams, heavy and mild
Render my thoughts horn y and vile.

And from your lips a tender kiss
Recalls to my mind what I miss.
There I remain in lonesome bore
Longing for your warmth and much more.

Just Because

Just because every living soul
The Lord creates
Silently hungers to be whole,
Seeking a mate,

Just because every free motion
Thus extended,
Is good or bad in reaction,
Forth intended.

Just because nature in the spring,
Appears renewed
Just because the night brings snoring,
Bad dreams all strewed.

Just because the golden sunshine
Brings happiness,
Just because with your hand in mine,
I feel no stress.

Just because on every tree branch,
Can a bird nests,
And that every given park bench
Can love, attests.

Just because every given brook
Quenches willows,
That all it took was just one look
For me to know

That all I needed in my life,
Genuine and true,
Was for you to decide and dive
And start anew.

To you only my thoughts aspire,
Mumbling your name
And my soul blazes in fire,
Your face to blame.

I send you silent well wishes,
Riding my love,
Praying that the Lord enriches
You with His Dove.

I send you all my ecstasy
With strolling dreams,
Each harboring a fantasy
Where you're the theme.

Yet still my mind has one island
With golden shore
Where it lingers, holding your hand
Like once before.

Receive my love, my angel fine,
For rainy days.
Your hand is already in mine,
Thus the Lord say.

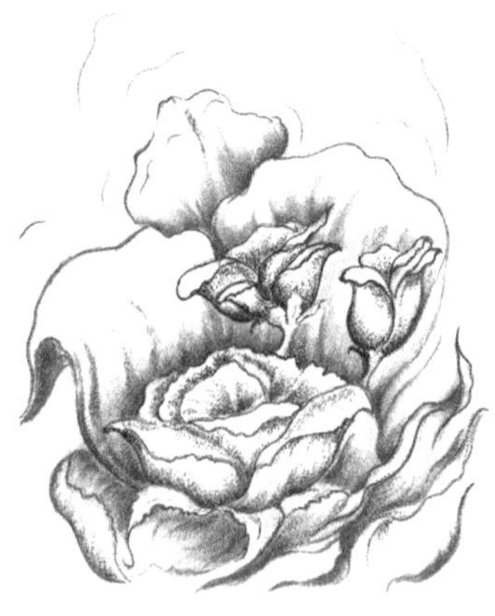

Her Song

Searching for you right from the start
Stopping us from being apart
And nothing else matters to me.
Holding you tight against my life,
Dissipating my inner strife
And all the rest is so petty.

I am the shoulder for your cross,
The toddler child whose mother's lost
In this large crowd of St James' fair,
I am the shadow on your wall
Who did not hear the morning call
And stayed caught in this love affair.

I am the fish out of your pond
Which stifles while you don't respond
To its desperate gesturing,
I am the sound within your ears
Resounding softly for it fears
To become whisper annoying.

Run My Letter

For an eternity
My heart has been lonely,
Finally it open'
To a jolly maiden.
It emerged suddenly from its hibernation
And is dying to love; carry its petition,
Run my letter, run.

Don't go on lingering,
Don't go mind your own thing.
You should get up and leave,
Ignore other missive'
Who occupy your time with their petty gossips
When they should deliver what is sealed with their lips,
Run my letter, run.

When she opens her eyes
Discerning your disguise,
Beg her to consider
The weight of my offer.
She'll read between your lines and detect at a glance
That my life without her will not stand any chance,
Run my letter, run.

Tell her I will always
Warm her nights, cheer her days.
Remind her that never
Will my feelings waver,
That my sun will always retire in her sea,
That I will always smile for her brown eyes to see.
Run my letter, run.

Daily Thoughts

Just like this year lilacs, stroked by the daring sun,
Whispering to the spring that its time is at hand,
The thoughts of you gently come ashore on my mind.

They come an gently lie exposing their tan buns,
Well aware of the seal they once lovingly brand'
On my soul they possess, the soul you left behind.

Someone spoke of recess; of this they give me none.
They're cherished and pampered so they treasure the sand,
This sand yearning for you all dejected and pined.

So like this year lilacs, rendered bold by the sun,
I cry out to you, this no one understands,
When thoughts of you, daily come and dock on my mind.

Pathways

Down the hallways of life, tread a man and his soul,
The hallways where we all struggle to take control
Of the ups and downs of living,
Of fate and love disheartening.
They talk in silent sobs of broken love affairs
Where words of forever and you and I don't pair.
But lightly they both tread
And their sadness is fed
By each and everyone with their soul that they meet,
Walking down the hallways bore by the same Spirit.

Down the pathways of life where we only meet once.
O life, O life, why do you still our loved ones?

PS

It's been a sheer blessing to have known in my life
A sweet angel like you, of gentleness so rife.

Thoughts...

I want to say so much
That I think you should know;
I love you...
I need you...
You're the sun of my night...
But in vain words I search
That could describe the glow
Around you,
Straight from you;
My thoughts put up a fight.

You'll never comprehend
How vulnerable I feel
With my heart in your hands
Making silent appeal
That you remain gentle,
Loving, kind and jolly,
Yet crazy a little
But not dilly-dally.

I caught myself worrying
Bout losing you one day;
Dreadful thoughts
Silly thoughts
That express of my heart
The depths of the feeling
From me coming your way;
Loving thoughts,
Merry thoughts
Wishing we never part.

Say

I long for you, I long for you.
Do you know how I long for you?
I long for you that all I do
Is mourn all the times I failed you.

I long for you all my days through
But say, do you do the same too?
My soul always reaching for you
Leaves me weary; I long for you.

Because You're My Baby

Because you're my Baby, I promise to be true,
To support all your dreams and share your worries too,
To be there when you call, try to see things your way,
And if it is your wish, away from you to stay.

Because you are my Boo, I will give you my trust,
The safeguard of my heart, whether you're wrong or just.
I'll make every attempt as to lessen your load,
Whenever you succeed I'll be there to applaud.

Because you're my Chérie, I will make you happy.
This world can be so mean, so cold and so snappy
But because I love you, your wounds I'll try to soothe
Since from all those beating it's my heart you will choose

To look on your brown eyes every time the dawn breaks,
To wager on your love even when life's at stake.
We'll finally grow old as though together be
Peas of a single pod…because you're my Baby.

Dreambound

All alone, when the sun depicts the horizon,
At this time when nature sheds its sweetest season,
The purple glare reclines, slowly fading away
While the yellow forest gold-plates all mountaintops,
The fall then skillfully sweet nature, photo shops
As if the sun and rain rusted all on their way.

Oh! For the love of God! Who has this magic hand,
That'd suddenly produce, not just only pretend,
While the shadows creep in from every known corner,
Next to me, in person, before glides in the moon,
The ever-real silhouette of my sweet Marijune
To complete this old sketch, next to me, the loner?

Let her come and instill deep within me the thrill
Of past autumn evenings, when she was the queen still.
Rekindle deep in me the love I hold so dear
While I bathe in the awe of this autumnal dusk
When in the air lingers a muttered touch of musk,
And I gaze in the thoughts of holding her so near.

Junedreaming

(Slumberings)

Daydreaming I pull you near
In my tub of lavender
Truly unable to steer
In or out of slumber.

In your sleepy thoughtfulness
I fade away silently.
Conversely my consciousness
Will see you or will see me.

Went back to catch up with you'
In the land of your sweet dream.
Nothing stays and nothing's true;
All come apart at the seams.

From either side of the bed
Every scene comes shine aglow
And the scent that lies ahead
In my mind resounds hollow.

Tenderly from dusk to dawn
I miss you in my embrace
And I'll be straw on your lawn
Till you breathe life in my face.

End Of Day

At the end of my day, slowly I take my load
Of peaceful sentiments I gained from completion
Of the burdens the world that day chose to unload
And put on my shoulders with no hesitation.

At the end of my day though I feel much alert
I perceive already my spirit all willing
To take its nightly stroll and leave behind inert
My all-weary body from daily chores battling.

Though I know tomorrow I will start all over,
I trust the sun will shine again on my meadow.
For to hope is to live and to live is never
Lose sight of any dream, come joy or come sorrow.

At the end of my day therefore, I don't despair
Knowing day after day the sun shines on the dew.
The only balm that soothes my body wear and tear
Is to open my heart and think freely of you.

Divine Touch

It's 2 am and as usual,
Alone in my room I brainstorm,
The dawn is stillborn but casual,
Nothing is out of the norm.

So normally you step right in,
With no warning but with great ease.
Since of my world you are the queen,
Then naturally I feel so pleased.

I can tell you with a few words
The shiver of soul experienced
But the truth will never be heard
Until you ponder its essence.

You are the clear and new mirror
Of the love I get from my Lord,
By far His sole ambassador,
Bearer of love and care galore.

You will always come nudge my soul
Despite the long miles between us,
The blessing bestow made us whole
Although the bond is not obvious.

How I Wish

The little joys that life bestows,
Like when I hold you in my arms.
The little joys erase the blows
When I fall, stricken by your charms.

The little thrills that I can sense,
Like when I hold your pretty face,
The thrilling ups and the descents
Roller coast my heart in its pace.

The many words you can whisper
Resound over within my mind,
But none can compare in flavor
To when you say you miss me blind.

Fool Or Sage

Call me a fool or call me a sage,
I will always dwell on the page,
This short page of my life story,
That tales of you and I, chérie.

Call me a fool or call me sage,
The mischiefs done in younger age
Always leave the heart wide open
For a sea of sorrow and pain.

I'll sit alone, empty, weary,
Chewing the regrets I carry.
And between shots I'll reminisce
Your precious love I always miss.

Call me a fool or call me sage,
My soul will stall right at this stage
Of searching always for his mate,
Humbled yet still proud of this fate

Of longing for you, my Honey;
This drive so strong and uncanny.
I will remain right in your cage,
Call me a fool or call me sage.

Morning Plight

This morning I held you so tight,
I could not, just could not let go.
I did not dream of you last night
But today is one-woman show.

My pillows annoyed by the scene
Did not cradle this déjà vu.
They think you're cold, they think you're mean,
They think, because they miss you too.

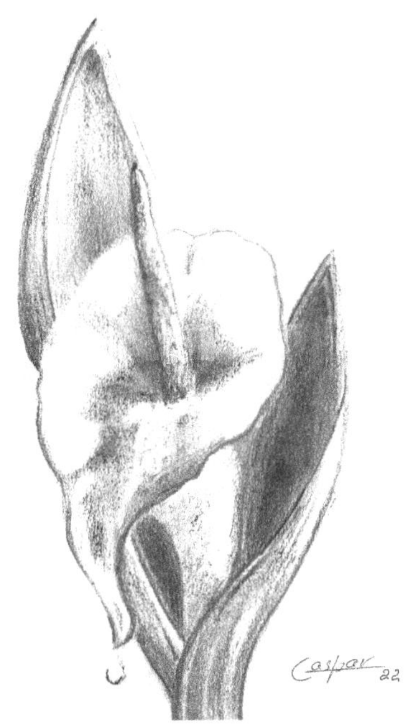

Regrets

Once upon in lifetime, as though to prove a point,
That the power of love still befalls the conjoint,
Two souls gladly surfing over this world's meadows,
Hand in hand, relieving one another's sorrow,
Glowing in blissful might, gleaming of the same light,
Emanating a sun, forever warm and bright,
Living one and the same, basking in sweet glory,
Dazzled, like exiting some enchanted story,
Where this pair of lovebirds, with borrowed rays of sun,
Would, in their ecstasy, the rest of us, just shun.
If ever they would be, from themselves drawn apart,
They'd resourcefully steer towards their counterpart
And in a sweet sudden, daring the daunting crowd,
Dash towards the other, then soar above the clouds…

Oh yes, I had once known, the true love of my life.
You dream of her embrace, so often and so true.
And at the crack of dawn, despite your fiercest strife,
She flies, leaving you her sweet dew.

You yearn for her return, down some flowery trail.
You send silent clamors, on your knees, night and day.
But when you hear the knock, sadly it never fails,
To be just a mirage that stray'.

And if in my weakness I were to let them in,
That would be, of my time, such a waste and a lost.
I'd pay for my beloved, with regrets deep within.
But remorse has a higher cost.

Don't call her name to me, don't rekindle the flame.
Don't speak of this old time when I was once complete,
For the sound of my voice never remains be the same,
When I remember my defeat.

Everyone deep inside harbors within their soul,
A lost love and so learned to stifle the deep sighs.
We all carry a cross, paying subtly a toll,
Once our chance has passed us by.

This love boat, in lifetime, only once docks your shore
Blessed is the pilgrim it finds keen and ready!
Whenever it departs, much loaded than before,
You suffer your loss already.

We sober silently; we make all kind of deals.
We beg for an encore, a replay of the scene.
But forward, we all go, nothing's at a standstill.
Only the Lord can intervene.

She flew my Tweedy Bird, without leaving a trace
But she sings in my heart at every crack of dawn.
And still at my window I hope to see her face,
Sweetly skipping upon my lawn…

Oh yes, I had once known, the true love of my life.
I dream of her embrace, so often and so true.
At each crack of my dawn, despite my fiercest strife,
I wake up missing her anew.

Gone Away

And here I am again at your doorsteps today,
All lonesome, despondent, pitiful as they say.
As if all a sudden an awful twist of fate
Would have sucked out of me the life I had of late.

No desire, no drive, no plan for the future.
A total heart and soul unfortunate rupture.
Deflated air balloon thrown in certain corner
Of which she, the toddler, became the disowner.

And here I am again wondering what's the use
To get out of bed. I cannot, I refuse
The offer of the friends so concerned and worried
Seeing my drive for life slip away, all harried.

Yes once again I stay all empty, dejected,
Not knowing what to do, if to do is fitted.
For only yesterday she was my living force,
My bearer of sunshine, my will-to-live the source.

But now that she eloped with no jotted reason,
The air within my chest, just like her, has long gone.
Nothing left to live for, not a heaven to pray.
That's why I'm here again at your doorstep to pray.

You're On My Mind

What a blissful delight to have you on my mind,
Painfully realize how much I miss you blind.
It comes to me always when I expect the least
And my poor heart bleeding gets me to clench my fist.

A loving heart remains a gift from God above.
Despite our failings He still shows us His love.
But in love we often fail to grasp one detail;
Of a coin love's the head and suffering the tail.

So love my lonely heart and then bleed thereafter,
Slowly you will favor the One of your Master.
For He loves steadily with nothing in return;
For your remote angel you have to bleed and yearn.

So I say I love you, my far away angel,
You who brighten my day and my dark night dispel.
For the blissful feeling to have you on my mind,
Though it lightens my load, makes that I miss you blind.

From Me To You

When it becomes all clear,
When the smoke is all gone
You will notice how near
You'll be to my person.

Just like me you waited
To reach this oasis,
This break long expected
Rendered your heart novice.

But you kept on your ground
And stuck to your standard,
When no solace you found,
Your hope, did not discard.

Then came that blessed eve
That saw your dream come true;
What you lost was retrieved,
In bundle sent to you.

Since now it is all clear
And your heart is renewed,
I can face all my fears
And declare I love you.

Return

I miss your lovely eyes and your beautiful smile,
I long to hear your voice resounding in my ears,
The softness of your hands; all for which my heart cheers
Causing that around you is where I want to while.

But in my heart, my love, the quivering reveal
The awful hours spent when you are not with me.
The days drag endlessly and deep inside I feel
The misery until you come back already.

But when you will return what will unveil my heart?
Speechless I will remain, quivering but jovial
And my eyes full of you, my lovely, better part,
Will they ever reveal my love to you at all?

But if ever my dear, you'd find me cold, distant,
Don't go making a scene with your mind wandering.
Remember that always away from you being,
I can't help my poor heart; I suffer and lament.

Sad Day, Blessed Day

The day will come but sadly so
When you'll immerse in your sorrow.
Some rainy day that'd come to stir
The lovely ones you had with her.

The memories will keep you warm,
All bundled up under her charm
But the pain of your heart bleeding
Will hurt as emotional sting.

In the vague stare of your wet eyes
You'll come sadly to realize
That you remain anchored easy
Down in the bottom of her sea.

But though bothered you will rejoice
To hear of your heart the strong voice
For only from a healthy heart
Strong love can pour though long apart.

Good Morning

Lying there next to me when the day's light and young
And the rest of the world their resting, still prolongs.
When the cares and worries, the plans and the deceits,
Nothing is yet ready to break down the spirits,

When I feel you reach out in the dark for my hand
While I wait and hope that my craving you'll attend.
When you slide in my arms to reclaim your abode
And right there, on your throne your emotions, reload.

When I can feel your heart talking straight into mine,
When your muffled pleasure, deep in your throat confined,
Seems to go hand in hand with your body's cadence
And my whole universe gladly joins in the dance.

When your hands so far shy gain in silent boldness
And I can feel your nails embedding in my chest.
When I perceive your breath short and warm on my face,
And your legs around mine intertwined for this race.

When we go unafraid, unaware of the clock,
Riding forbidden skies, hand with hand interlocked,
That finally we land upon the mute pillows
Conniving and muffling this escapade echo.

Then I tenderly hold you right against my chest,
Consciously cradling you, lovely bird of my nest.
And right between the breaths that we're barely taking,
Between hugs and kisses I whisper: "Good morning!"

Life Without You

Life without you is feasible,
Life without you is possible.
I live because I can wake up
I eat; I sleep and go to work,
Because I play, go to the gym
By my thorough check up it seems
That all is well, that I'm alive.

I live so far because I breathe,
Filling the air with my poor waste
While the rest of the world in haste
Misses that I'm all dead inside
Because you are not by my side.

Life without you is feasible
But I still remain disable.
True that I'm a registered voter,
True that I have a bank account,

True that I have a brand new name
To the others I'm just the same.
I greet people, smiling at times
Barely hiding what goes inside;
Stifling because I'm without you.

Life without you though feasible,
Life without you is horrible.
I go mingle with the others,
I give advice on tough matters,
I help around but all the while
I die daily behind a smile
Surviving carrying the load
Of somber days and lonely nights
Making up my lifeless living
That I die living without you.

Wise Advice

To forget me, don't intend; it's futile.
I will always be this fly on your wall.
I'll spring out at the least of the while
Each time from life you get bitter bile
And you would wish you could give me a call.

It's futile to forget me, don't intend.
I will come when you least expect and knock,
Cause a blank stare and your partner, offend.
More than often you will have to contend
With the sweet-you-and-I's mental block.

Don't intend. It's futile to forget me.
When alone in your room I'll approach you
Your eyes wide shut, feeling warm and clammy,
Your inner voice will see no infamy
When we embrace claiming our love anew.

So when all down and out you'll reach
For my old pic with smiling stare,
Know that this stifling bout is shared
Each time on my mind you so breach.

Midnight

(The night)

And the keyboard morose
Resounds the artist's song.
It's always one of those
Speaking of love so strong.

And the smokes permeate
All corners of the room.
You don't need any date,
Just your drink and your gloom.

For the notes in the air
Recall the past affairs.
Since we are no more pair,
The reveries are all Claire's.

But soon after day breaks
You'll face again the plight,
That old truth that still aches…
But now enjoy the night.

People

People come and people go,
Often it's a one-man show.
The one by your side today
Can always just fade away.

People come and people go
In your life like an arrow
Leaving in the aftermath
You, with heart of sociopath.

People come and people go;
Feels at time like a low blow
To grasp the cold-hearted fact
Numbing you like an infarct.

People come and people go
Worming their way in sorrow
When they're made to realize
They've been preyed before their eyes.

People come and people go
Then you're back to ground zero;
All the years you've invested
Leave your mouth bitter tasted.

People come and people go
Often leaving deep sorrow;
The air they displace with them
Leaves you stifling just the same.

People come and people go
That is as far as I know.
But then after they retreat
Study the message that's fit.

Since my sunshine has returned
And made all things so brand new,
I promise in fair return
To sunbathe and treasure you.

People come and people go
Making life dull and hollow
But thank God for destiny,
It's time for you my Junie.

And just like the breeze that blows
Bringing sunshine, bringing snow,
For as long as it echoes,
People will come and will go.

Just A Thought

And so there'll be, in days ahead,
A flow of love running with stead
From my heart to you, my Chérie.

You opened up its every door
And unlike anything before
Its ticking's fierce and yet merry.

Once in a while, when He beckons,
The Lord gives blessings in seconds
To rearrange a stagnant life.

Then all grateful, down on my knees,
I beg of you, O baby, please,
Will you accept to be my wife?

Hopeful

For one day with no fuss
We will reach other shore,
On day with no circus,
One day we'll cry no more.

It will come silently
Next to us take its place,
It will nudge us softly
To remind us the grace

That so long we hoped for
Crushed by this world around
Demanding more and more
From this love that we found.

For they perceived the bliss
That brought us thrill galore,
They surely did not miss
The glow not there before.

For when the heart's merry
The face displays the glow.
Love came in no hurry,
Ridded us of sorrow.

So one day with no glitz
Next to us will be calm,
No more John, Dawn or Fritz,
We will have no more qualms.

Loving You

I'll love you forever no matter where you are,
I'll love you forever, be it near, be it far.
I'll love you forever; this is what I live for
I'll love you when you'll be nothing but just a core.

My heart has forever beaten to your cadence,
It remains ectopic without your radiance.
I'll love you forever till you leave our midst
I'll love you still after you will cease to exist.

True Love

Love blinds the jolly heart;
Brought by old Cupid's dart,
Intoxicating the senses,
Tearing down the inner fences
Built over experience
Of all the tangos danced.

Love tames the fickle heart,
Snuggling its every part,
With themes of blue sky in April,
With hopes as when we were little.
Therefore the heart in trance
Forgives any offence.

Love soothes the bleeding heart
In ways much more too smart
For us the knowledge to fathom
And store in our safe bottom.
It's given in a glance
By Divine Providence.

You Again

Here you are in my arms again
Steady as a summer refrain,
Lovely and cheery like the fall.
Here you are in my world anew,
My clouds your sunshine pierced right through,
You must have heard my silent call.

Here you are in my arms again
My composure I can't regain
Bathing in the bright of your smile.
You returned to take possession
And my sorrows make concession
Of what they claimed for a long while.

Here you are again in my arms.
Succumbing to you jolly charms
Nothing can be ever sweeter.
Sweaty palms and palpating heart
Pierced again by your subtle dart
Of angel liking man-eater.

Oh damn you! Right into my life
You come to settle any strife
That might have rattled my status
Of lonely dude ever kissing
The lips that so long been missing
To which he held on mordicus.

Here you are, here you are, but how
Did you realize that the vow
I made not to date was serious?
It's just that always when in cage
The heart ignores any visage
Different from that of its Precious.

Here you are and what a pleasure
That you still remember Roger;
He wouldn't have stopped wagging its tail.
He took it harder your absence,
He suffered, suffered in silence
Even causing its heart to fail.

But here you are inquiring;
No flowers at your welcoming.
There were none in my icy land.
The rare buds in my entourage
Were sadly always a mirage
And the sun was never at hand.

But here right in my life again
You come back your throne to regain,
Victorious queen of lonely heart,
Now that you replanted your flag
To the whole world you can go brag
But from mine please cease to depart.

Take Over

My state of mind is in peril,
It suffered a coup to its state.
A coup d'état as it stood still,
A coup d'état to seal its fate.

My state of mind's no more a state.
It now has become a province,
A province annexed to your fate,
Your fate that now has my last chance.

My state of mind therefore will be
A mere image of your caprice.
Wherever you travel you'll see
All sites branded by you I miss.

Speechless

The many words I cannot find
Come play in meadows of my mind
Heralding the reality
That you're now my eternity.

The many words I cannot find
Though unspoken, they fall behind
And watch my heart dragged on a leash
By your sweet name that I cherish.

The many words I cannot find
Will never see, they are too kind,
The calm effect that on my sea
Your words impress, O my chérie.

I sit and slowly take the thrill
That your love to my heart instills.
It's unique and disrupts always
My peace of mind, my end of days.

The many words I cannot find
When thoughts of you run through my mind
Pronounce what I long discovered
That I will be yours forever.

If

If every word I speak their meaning could reveal,
If every thought I have could depict a picture,
If every sigh I breathe could transmit my appeal
They would forever be of you, my lost treasure.

If every hand I hold could be warm and tender,
If every one I hug, remain in my embrace.
If in my solitude I would fail to ponder
Over the many years since I last saw your face,

If every rising day, if every call I get,
Every mail I open, every time the bell rings,
If every one I greet, every one I upset,
Every one I care for, if every song I sing,

If my life as a whole would summarize a theme;
It would have for certain the liken of you, Dear.
But if again the Lord work at some divine scheme,
You will return my Love, to dry away my tears.

Come

Come, come, come to me
And I will tell you
Every ounce of pain
The soul can obtain
When he finds himself
Without the soul mate
That he so adores

Come, oh come and see
And I will show you
The hellish desert
That he had to cross
Knowing that he lost
The only creature
Born to his measure.

Come, come already
And appraise the trance
That only your eyes,
His most precious prize,
Can instill in him…
That's the silent scream
Of his love for you.

Wise Thoughts

I wish one day to let you know
How much I miss your lovely face
And hunger for your warm embrace

And then in turn hear the echo
Of your heart whispering to me
Words of angelic melody.

For senselessly we hold inside
Confessions of a bleeding heart,
Impulses felt right from the start.

Often the words stifled with pride
Remained sealed in our bosom
When with no clue our time comes.

My Ikigai

Alone when I frantically walk
In the troubling maze of my thoughts,
Reclined yet puzzled and distraught
By all the reason-why's I stalk,
The ones behind all my have-not's,

There, in the mirror of my fate,
I see a man devoid and poor,
Crushed and drowning in the downpour
Of griefs crashing on the estate
Of his world like never before.

I taste the once-upon-a-time's,
I feel the hands that slipped away.
I still can hear in my mind's sleigh
The sound of my past Christmas chime
Resonate like it was today.

But in the sadness rising high,
In this, cause of all my torments,
My hopes remain tranquil, dormant,
Not once troubled by the gray sky
Overcasting my firmament.

Upon this sphere where I stifle
Mourning her hand resting in mine,
The halo of my angel fine
Redirects the care I shuffle
Going through my long idyll line.

Sure I remain the lone ranger
Searching for the sole companion,
The one to ward off the danger
Lurking whenever a stranger
Comes to trip my dedication.

As it's been so long decided,
Any soul has only one mate.
About this there is no debate.
My heart's been steadily guided
By her light glow soft and innate.

Alone therefore, I change the tune
And frankly, right out of my vault,
I quickly reach and press default
To safely land on sandy dune
And hug again my Marijune.

Just Because It's Fall

I know just what you like, I know what you abhor.
I know what makes you sad and what you will fight for.
I know what tickles you, how much you love the fall,
And I know that's the time when I'll receive your call.

It's the best of seasons, when the sun always seems
To send to us its strong but rendered mellow beams.
It will shine then that day as to not to molest
You on the path you'll take, on the way to your nest.

You will return to me and Nature will approve.
The cushion of the leaves even your steps will soothe.
And the trees disrobing their precious apparel
Will tell you to restart, with no fuss, with no bell.

No wonder we name it the season of advent;
It's the time to prepare for most precious events,
Like the birth of a Child, the rebirth of Nature,
And the recovering of lost precious treasures.

So you'll return to me in the midst of the fall,
Your favorite season, I faithfully recall.
Because I know you well, oh yes, this I can tell,
You will reclaim your boo, with no fuss, with no bell.

Magic Touch

I often sit alone, slowly just taking in
The silent euphoria surging from deep within
When thoughts of you emerge, in a blissful sudden,
Relieving magically whatsoever burden.

You come so silently and with your gentle touch,
Always without a clue, to give ease to my rush.
There, alone in this truce, I feast on the meaning
Of how much I love you and many other things.

But the thoughts I harbor, to one thing often lead:
How lucky I've become since my psyche you feed.
Love has landed in me the day I first met you,
You have planted in me the seed of love so true.

You are my Eureka, the genie of my lamp,
No wonder on my mind so frequently you tramp.
When I feel invaded by this loving feeling,
That's when I sit alone and slowly take all in.

Babe

I promised I would pray
For love to come my way…
And then came you

I promised I would love
The way my Lord above
Taught me to do.

For gazing in your eyes
I deeply realize'
My dreams came true.

Silently then I say
To the Lord whom I pray
Merci beaucoup.

Reminiscing

The Sunday glare, lovely and bright,
So lowly fades from East to West
And all creatures with healthy sight
Seemingly empty up their chests

From burden galore they carry,
From unexpected frustrations,
From errands run in a hurry
Which robbed them the Sunday notion;

This day of rest, this day of truce
This day to gather in good will
To hear and ponder on the truths
Which hold the world foundation still.

But I remain, on this good day,
Wrapped up in full reminiscence.
For always then you come my way,
You who shine despite your absence.

The lovely Sunday glare was bright,
In all hearts ignited a cheer.
But all the while, though out of sight,
You kept my heart throbbing my Dear.

Love's Coin

For it's only when the heart bleeds
That you're aware that you're in love.
It's only when love plants its seeds
That your soul fits hers like a glove.

So you stifle when you're alone
For you miss the air that she breathes.
Since your will to live is all gone
Your emotions are put to freeze.

For you're shivering all inside
Lacking the warmth of her presence
And swallowing your foolish pride
You call and call with insistence.

And you go on to perpetrate
The smallest of her daily acts.
This feeds the never-ending state
Of good times you want to bring back.

But don't despair, oh don't be sad,
Rejoice instead and pray it lasts,
This case is far from being bad;
It's healthy for the heart to fast.

Only then you become aware
Of the depths of the love you share.
I know, my friend, it is not fair
But love stings when you truly care.

So go, nurture your achy heart,
Yearn day and night, and night and day,
Yearn for the hand of your sweetheart
Deep in your heart she'll always stay.

And as often, before you know,
Before your feelings consume you
Around you she'll joyfully throw
Her embrace fed by love so true.

For only when the soul withers
You are aware of where you stand.
Rejoice then that your heart suffers
The two extremes that love commands.

Charade

The gloom over me hazing
Grimaces at every tone
Of this tune I try to sing.
Like when majesty's dethrone'
The court then does its own thing.

Sadly there's not a fiber
Not an ounce, in nowadays
To slip a shade of laughter.
But hope is a dawn away
To the faithful believer.

No need to misplace the goal
That faithful prayer will reach.
There will always be a toll.
The believer finds a breach
If he looks deep in his soul.

But never there is a need
To holler the naked truth,
It is well known in its seed.
The fairy needs just one tooth
To spread around her good deeds.

Sipping slowly at this gall
You will taste the love you miss
But won't hear her silent call
For alone in your abyss
You can see dusk slowly fall.

Always in other quarters
Short of rain there is blue sky.
Staring down the hereafter
You can see your life zoom by,
No time left for your barter.

Right there, class, gender and race
All aspects of divergence
On your screen come show their face.
Every so upheld difference
Of importance lost all trace.

This song I refrain deep down
Well caught up within my cage
To my neighbor brings a frown
For every willful hostage
To the world favors a clown.

Nothing in life is secure.
You may win or you may lose.
But always what you endure,
To the gander or the goose,
Offer as sheer literature.

Love hides no cacophony
Once it invites us to dance.
Blessed are the so many
Who at its treasure took glance;
For this I thank my Junie.

Knight's Sight

And from within the night
Rendered cold by the fright,
Deep from within the night
You set on me your sight.

And all of a sudden
As in a fairy tale,
But in such a sudden
I became much less pale.

So then you took my hand,
Got me up on my feet.
I held on to your hand,
Afraid to leave my seat.

But you smiled tenderly,
Honest and loving soul,
Then giggled merrily
But did not dare lose hold

Of my poor lonely heart
Longing for a soul mate,
That one heart set apart
That'd come and change its fate…

But from within my night,
Despite my dreaded fright
You came and set things right
Once on me you set sight.

Melancholy

The door swings wide open
And the sun permeates
Down to the empty plates
We dined in so often.

Far in the sky you see
The lengthy trail of clouds
Left weekly by the proud
Air force dignitaries.

Upon the mountain tops,
Shining loud, shining red,
The villas haughty stead
Show the pride of their props.

And since it's almost ten
You will hear moo the cows
Which an hour will plow
Wishing for eleven.

See how nothing has changed;
The wind bends the branches,
The rain the birds, drenches
But only have estranged
The roses you planted
From this forsaken place.
Like you they left no trace,
Not at all contented…

Funny how without fail,
With deepest displeasure,
The ones you so treasure
Away from your docks, sail…

Just Your Smile

Some want money, others pleasure,
Others want both in no measure.
Some pray for health on lonely beds
While others waste their own instead.

Some prefer to work for their needs,
Others their laziness they feed.
Some go through this life with a frown,
While others daily play the clown.

And yet others in solitude
Worship their God in plenitude,
Whereas a few, along remain
Because they so hate their brethren.

While so many keep their mouth shut
Others talk so you'd think their nut…
It's always this solid refrain
Tearing the world in its domain.

But I only, once in a while,
Long for your jolly, lovely smile…
Nothing on earth is more pleasing
Than to know that it's my causing.

I Could

I could bombard you with my thoughts,
Reveal the many times I sought
Of your hand and mine tie the knot,
Live happily after.

I could dismantle all the norms,
The ones society transforms,
In jail so humans can perform
Like birds of one feather.

I could tear down every barrier
And get our hearts so merrier,
Leaving a life so much freer,
You for me, me for you.

I could pulverize the concept,
The ones that got you to accept
Subtly society precepts
Upheld your whole life through.

Only I rather, my sweet dove,
Just pray daily that your sweet love
Be sent to me right from above
Bind us one another.

The Last Day

The last day I saw you I can never forget.
We had said everything, we were ready and yet
There was this sense of doom, this feel of end of days,
This choking sensation of what I'll have to pay.

The last day I saw you, for some unknown reason,
I could perceive the price that would cost my treason.
But since I had to choose a trail way for my heart,
I opted painfully for my belle to depart.

The last day I saw you was the last day I smiled.
The last day I saw you stayed with me a long while.
Repeatedly I dream of this crime to undo,
Repeatedly I dream instead, of choosing you.

The last day I saw you therefore I will retain,
I'll keep it till one day, atonement I obtain.
And hopefully, just as the balance I upset,
The purging of my soul this offense, will offset.

My Junebug

And I love you still
My stifling heart you fill
Thoughts of you soothe my ills
And I thank God for you

People don't understand
That I can take your hand
By closing my eyes and
Relive our life anew.

But yes, I know
It's on my private screen
That I play all these scenes
And it's feeding my sorrow.

But I won't let
These memories just depart
They feed my very heart
And it's my only outlet.

But do you love me still,
Is my battle uphill,
Have you long my fate sealed?
I pray God that's not so.

For when I hear your name
My heart still leaps the same
For my spirit you tame,
Just like him… I don't know.

Last Breath

Even the last breath I exhale
Will be meant to call on your name.
It will emerge fragile and pale,
Bearing your colors just the same.

The life you live seeking a hand,
Seeking a hand firmly to hold,
Appears to you empty and bland
When you're feeling weary and cold.

So for the last time I will look
On my screen, my life flashing by,
Painfully mourning that it took
This tragedy for you to try

To grace my room with your presence,
And finally offer hand,
This hand I sought as a last chance,
Just when my chance comes to an end.

So my last breath I will exhale
Peacefully calling out your name
Just to summarize the sad tale
Of a life spent seeking your flame.

Under Your Spell

The song you sang to my Master
Got Him helpless under your charms.
In return, He then ministered
And brought my soul into your arms.

So here I am forever yours,
All too resigned, all so happy.
This chase will soon come to a close.
We'll touch hands; it won't be sappy.

And so it will reveal to all,
Despite slips, tumbles and all odds,
That love always stands straight and tall
Around those who put trust in God.

My love for you will not falter.
It grew solid from your absence.
My heart became ever fonder
Slowly simmered in your essence.

Never will I in my lifetime,
Never, for I looked all over,
Never will I, in this lifetime,
Feel like this for any other.

Love Struck

I stand here facing this blank wall,
The blank wall of my very mind.
I just stand here feeling so small,
Searching for words I cannot find.

The many times that from my chest
Surges this well-known tsunami,
I repeatedly failed the test
Of finding words hidden in me.

Meanwhile this feeling consuming
My heart and soul all the way through,
Gives no recess to my being.
It surges with the thoughts of you.

Relentlessly I try to stick
A noun or epithet to it
But as always they come too weak,
Never full of loving spirit.

I bang my head on this blank wall
But nothing ever comes to save
The day. But all I can recall
Is your embrace for which I crave.

So I remain alone, stranded
In this, the quicksand of your love
Leaving my words empty handed
And useful meanings ridded of.

So there I stand facing this wall,
All kept in your love that spellbinds,
My words don't stand a chance at all;
Miserably they trail behind.

Darkest Hour

Ah! So sweet the nothings, so true the endearments
Uttered by my Junie, chasing all my torments!
Spirits of the nineties, who tested our romance,
Have you pleaded with God to give us one more chance?

The years were so young yet, but the wills were so strong.
New york shined in the fall, Doylestown still belong'
To the fervent Christians at every first Friday.
Clearwater yet remained far, far away at bay.

The plans were so steady and the hearts so willing.
All seemed to be arranged, none that'd still need nailing.
The horizon afar seemed day by day closer;
No doubts were on the minds, the world knew I chose her.

Before the Lord of love we planned to seal it all.
Twas all said, twas all done from what I still recall.
But in a cruel sudden came the unthinkable;
The cold blade in the back, our plans to disable.

And all came tumbling down, and ever since remained
All tarnished, damp and cold, with soul forever stained.
But He who sees the heart in its true contrition,
In mercy will restore all to His volition.

Therefore the faith remains, as blind as faith can be.
Strong enough to sustain, strong enough to foresee
The ingenious plan of the good Lord of Hosts
From whom nothing escapes, even tricks of cheap ghosts.

Patiently

Come the days and go the nights
Quietly
My world tiptoes on the trace
Silently,
The trace fresh and the trace bright
Of my jolie,
Still longing for her embrace
Patiently.

You, drive of my every breath,
Come and see
The gaiety my heart ignores
Painfully.
Ever since my world you left
Suddenly,
My sea froze missing your shores
Patiently.

Patiently, sweet theme of my war,
Waged in my heart, waged in my soul,
Waged while chasing my shinny star,
Patiently my most cherished scar
Brand me for life but take me whole
For I am yours thus far.

Come back and rekindle my life
Joyfully
Come and steer my drifting boat
To safety,
Escort me on my last path
Rightfully,
Come and my sadness demote.
Patiently.

I see sunlight, I see rain
Equally,
I see love flourish abound
Cheerfully
Though I suffer now the pain
Tragically
Still I'll wait till you're around
Patiently.

Lovely

Lovely, you're so lovely,
As lovely as a rose.
Lovelier than the blue sky
After a summer rain,
Lovely as the Heavens
With a clear rainbow tie.
Lovelier than a starry night,
A humming bird in its still flight.

Lovely, but so lovely,
Lovely under the rain.
Lovely as a strong need
You're just about to feed.
As lovely as the sheets
Of lovers in retreat,

As lovely as the night
Caught by the dawn's first light.
As lovely as a child
In all his innocence,
As lovely as our love
Given this blessed chance,
As lovely as the eve
Of your first Christmas day,

As lovely and as fine
As the day you'll be mine.
Lovely, lovelier than before,
As lovely as the sun rising,
Lovely as though tribulating
You would've come out lovelier.
Lovely, so full of loveliness,
All emanating from your chest.

You seem to be so damn lovely
That I stand watching stunningly.
As lovely as the break of dawn
On a dejected spirit's lawn.
So you'll remain just as lovely
From the dawn till the end of day
You the one and you the only
Bringer of bright smiles and sunrays.

My Grace

In the blank stillness of my night,
You come steady, you come solely.
From deep within my silent plight
I long for your hand, my lovely.

Nothing has ever felt so warm,
Nothing so far's been so mellow,
Nothing can my anger, disarm
Better than your sweet voice echo.

The love you feed on the wire
Comes rushing down into my veins.
It ignites this blazing fire
Consuming me, heart, spirit, brain.

It keeps me warm when nights are cold,
Gives me great strength to carry on,
Provides a cozy but strong hold
When my spirit feels like a ton.

You come but one never knows how
You will affect me on that day.
But rest assured, before you bow,
Easily you dispel my gray

And delighted by the effect
I go on singing through my day.
The infusion is so direct
That nothing can get in its way.

So from the depths of my cold night
I come again to kiss your hand
And suddenly it's warm and bright,
Something the world can't comprehend.

Mirages

In all honesty I'll reveal
To you what's bugging me, my friend.
I'll let you know if you sit still,
About this great matter at hand.

The knock of opportunity
Deep in the heart resounds often
But sometimes sheer insanity
Is the rationale you obtain.

What may seem or sound so perfect,
What could be the best of option,
What could be coming so direct
Can be a solid delusion.

You tend to see just what you want,
What deep in your heart you desire,
But please, don't you be ignorant
Of its generated fire.

Always proceed with great caution,
Never jump and act too early.
Always leave room for discretion,
Never have one exit only.

Listen to the Spirit in you,
Your silent but sure leading voice.
He guides always with Love that's true
And directs you to the right choice.

Mirage will come, mirage will go,
Most of the time bringing sorrow.
Keep in mind that as they do so
The right one's coming tomorrow.

Loving You

(Amarte a ti)

Loving you is not the best, this I know for sure,
Having so many things to do less traumatizing,
Like finding faces in the clouds,
Like going to the movies or doing nothing.

Loving you is not the best but I like it.
Maybe I'm playing as always at being masochist,
Instead of entertaining myself with soccer
Or with the Internet like every one does.

Loving you is not the best but it's perfect
For it gives some sense to this routine
Of being always only a citizen, only just that.

Loving you makes me suffer, but I am so fortunate.
For it reminds me that I exist and that I feel,
For it gives me something to think about all night long, makes me alive.

Loving you is venom that gives life.
It's a torch that brightens up when turned off.
It's the sublime coupling the nonsense,
It's a feeling; therefore who'd understand?
Loving you is the most fabricated truth.
It's the best of the worst I've ever experienced.
It's Russian roulette for a kiss,
It's just so unpredictable.

Loving you is an error, a friend told me.
He believes that being happy is being free
But fails to understand the thrill of the unknown.

Loving you is a flickering moment in my mind,
It's also having hated you now and then,
Loving you is just absurd and we both know it
But it'll stay this way…as long as it lasts.

Shiny Star

Where have they gone, the sunny days,
Those days I had you in my arms?
Where are those warm and golden days
When I had you and all your charms?

I sit often just to exhale
Each time I scan what we've become.
But now I put my heart for sale
And roam, nonchalantly lonesome.

There will be days of clouds so low,
There will de days deprived of dew.
There will be days that will echo
The destiny of my and you.

But all the while through the dark nights,
The cold storm, the rainy seasons,
Always your halo strong and bright
Leads me steady, helps me live on.

I miss my warm and sunny days
With glow borrowed straight from your eyes.
I miss you whose spirit I pray
To come back and brighten my skies.

My High Noon

Like the desert under high noon
I burn in the wait of your love
Hoping that it would be here soon
To gladly brighten my alcove.

You spread your wings over my soul
And in my chest where it simmers,
My love, all robed in red and gold,
Over my world spreads its glimmers.

You'll never guess what has become
My whole life caught within your sphere.
You'll never guess just how gruesome
My heart can feel without you, dear.

Amid the treasures I cherish
Your face shines like the purest gold.
With kisses daily I polish
The best asset that I behold.

Like the desert under high noon
You consume my heart from above.
I will remain, singing your tune
Patiently waiting for your love.

My Reverie

Like the passionate dawn with its golden brushes,
Over Mother Nature sketches a look of hope,
Like a tune overheard, the inner soul touches,
Like a toddler in tears after Mommy elopes,

Like the Nor'easter wind before the frigid rain,
Like the smile of a child when his mother returns,
Like the dusk puts an end to every bird refrain,
Like golden wheat meadows that daily the sun burns,

Like the mysterious sea safeguards all her treasures,
Like a twiddling of birds early at break of dawn,
Like a grain quickly springs from favorable pasture,
Like the lonely beetle on the fairest of lawns,

Like every flower buds surrounded by its thorns,
Like the light butterfly straight from its chrysalis,
Like a genuine champion the trophy sought, adorns
Like the stamp of the years the forehead cannot miss,

Like the sea and the sky merge at the horizon,
Like the flow of gossip from weekly newspaper,
Like the birds flying south at the winter season,
Like the end of an air by a soloist tapered,

Like a skiff in distress that mighty waves cradle,
Like the divine reply of a fervent prayer,
Like a lonely puppet that clever hands fiddle,
Wrapped around your finger, be my skillful player.

Like every broken heart a blessed day will mend,
Like a snowy winter precedes a lovely spring,
Like a contrite sinner his flaws tries to amend,
My heart, my soul, my self, all at your feet I bring.

None Else More

Open your ears, lovely maiden, open your ears,
Open your ears so his serenade you can hear,
Open your ears; this is your beggar standing here;
Him alone, none else more.

Open your ears, my lady fair, open your ears
He comes daring, from her sweet dream, his angel steer,
He comes ado declaring his love to you, dear,
You alone, none else more.

Open your eyes, my angel fine, open your eyes,
Open your eyes and see in him there's no disguise.
Open your eyes and of his heart come see the size
Beat for you, none else more.

Open your eyes, my tweedy bird, open your eyes,
Open your eyes; he comes out loud so please arise.
Open your eyes for here alone he feels chastised
By you and none else more.

Open your door, O my sunshine, open your door,
Open your door and like you've never done before
Receive the love that on this night he comes to pour
At your feet, none else more.

Open your door, my sweetie pie, open your door,
Open your door; hear his voice to the heavens soar.
This night is cold but thoughts of you, whom he adores,
Comfort him, none else more

Heaven and Earth, lovely Pumpkin, Heaven and Earth
Are here tonight, of this love, to bless the rebirth.
Open your heart, for much too long he missed your mirth,
Cuddle and so much more.

Main Squeeze

I will not attempt to tell you
The load of thoughts submerging me.
I won't even hint to your view
The lines my queries carved deeply

On my forehead trying to hide,
To keep the world free of worries,
The pressing matters deep inside,
The ones fueling my dream series…

The part of me you've always been,
That part my other part treasures,
The part I'd seek through thick and thin,
That part source of all my pleasures.

That part in me I keep alive,
That part leads me in all I do.
For all I do in this here life
Shows the love I partake with you.

I will therefore keep well concealed
The many words I could tell you
For they carry sadness and thrill
Depending on your psyche too.

You will always know what I feel,
You will always dictate my mood,
You will always come and reveal
To my mind when it's time to brood.

My Sunrise

This morning I held you so tight,
I could not, just could not let go.
I did not dream of you last night
But today it's one-woman show.

My pillows annoyed by this scene
Did not cradle this déjà vu.
They think you're far, far, not yet seen,
They think… because they miss you too.

It was so strong, it was so real,
It was the best I've ever had,
It was the way you made me feel
That left me stirred but left me sad.

So I got up and naturally
On paper I let run my thoughts.
What is written is meant solely
To let you know how much I'm caught

In this early one-woman show,
Following my long, lonely night.
There I meet my little swallow
And get to hold her so, so tight.

Your Eyes # 2

When I look in your eyes I see my horizon.
So many times before I gazed in other skies
But like deer to water I come back to reason
And return faithfully to you, my lovely prize.

So many times before I have tried willingly
To leave their peaceful glow and lively tenderness
But always I return to your arms my jolie,
Happy to be your own, with loving eagerness.

They remain the mirror, in which I size my world,
They reflect the fervor of the love in your heart.
They are the loving cause my love for you unfurled.
They are now the reason we cannot stay apart.

Your eyes, my darling dear, remain my horizon.
More than enough I gazed into different skies.
But just like a swallow chasing better season,
Faithfully I come back, spellbound by your brown eyes.

Sweeter Than You

Sweeter than you, kinder than you,
I traveled far, as far can be,
Searching, searching for someone who
Would dare swim the troubled sea
Your candid heart dared to sail through.

Sweeter than you, but tell me who
In this lifetime has ever thought
That in your stead, unique, brand new,
Nobody else so far has brought
This love as sweet as honeydew.

Sweeter than you, all this life through,
With words and knees bent at your feet,
Though far away I search ado,
Faithfully I'll wait for my treat
And live this love that I once knew.

My Obsession

From the first beam of sun till the birds sing no more,
From the early babble of my still dreamy mind,
From the Morning Prayer and the plans I restore,
From the galloping thoughts that my concern rewinds,
You linger on my mind, morning, evening and night.

From the glass of water showering my heartache,
From the cup of coffee sent my spirit to perk,
From the first bite I take only my fast to break,
From the first word I say at home or when at work,
Despite any milieu, my spirit holds you tight.

There is never a truce, never a dull moment,
Never an occasion to be sad and lament.
You entertain my mind with the words you utter,
You entertain my soul with your playful laughter.

From the good folks I meet, the ones who so worry,
From the work that I do light-hearted and grateful
From the many missing the why I'm so merry,
From all the thanks I give towards the Merciful,
In my somber journey, remain my guiding light.

My Muse

When I sit alone with my thoughts,
When I empty my daily load,
When from all the goals that I sought,
The ones that popped up on my road,

My mind sizzles in hot debate,
When I go search down my alleys
The reasons crushing down my fate
But come with nothing but follies,

When finally I can affront
My old pucker in the mirror
Knowing that all the dos and don'ts
Were handled with tact and honor,

When the concerns this world offers,
The ones I ponder all day through,
Seem to overtake the laughter
Charging our stamina anew,

Then you surface with all your charm,
Quintessence of all reveries,
Bringing to my soul in alarm
A sucker to ease my worries…

Always then when I sit alone
Of my concerns I'm not afraid
Knowing that once you're on your throne
My petty thoughts and care just fade.

My Treat

Come, my sweet baby, come,
Come rest your weary feet.
Up and down, time and some,
You've been with my spirit.

My mind remains under
The control of my will
But my spirit hovers
Ocean, valley and hill.

It follows you always,
Worries when you don't smile,
Watches over your ways,
Stays with you all the while.
You remain of my dreams
The skillful conductor
And in my days, it seems,
The symphonies linger.

What a divine feeling
To have you as insight.
You keep my day gleaming,
Inspire my deep night.

Come then, my jolie, come,
Come here and be my treat.
Too long I was lonesome,
My soul, come and complete.

This Woman

There is this woman whom I love,
All dressed in red, all dressed in white
The smile she bears reminds me of
Childhood Christmas and silent night.

There is this woman whom I love
With eyes where lies sheer tenderness,
Tenderness of a lovely dove,
A lovely dove fresh from the nest.

So here's the woman whom I love,
Lovely, serene yet strong and kind.
Rain, snow or shine from up above,
Nothing can get her off my mind.

My Reasons Why

I will forever be, as far as I can see,
I will forever be contented but lonely.
The seeds planted in me if I want them to grow,
Carefully, peacefully, I'll have to go solo

Not that I so treasure the echo of my voice,
Not that I did not pray to have another choice
But the more I observe of my room the stillness,
The more I understand the pros of loneliness.

Regardless of the way your miseries befall
They surely at the end bring about your true call
And when you turn around pondering on your past
You slowly decipher the reasons why at last.

This poem does not provide to the mislead reader
Any moral license for carefree life manner,
But just by accepting the weaknesses in you
Then you benefit from the Spirit's Might in you

Carefully, peacefully I'll have to go solo
Until straight to my ears her voice will come echo.
But until that morning, as far as I can see,
With the Spirit in me, contented I will be.

PS

By standing humbly in His sight,
All your wrongs the Lord will make right.
Gently put your hand in His hand,
One day your life you'll comprehend.

Your Heart

Like an ass led to market fair
With carrot stick up in the air
So relentlessly I reach for
Your heart that I so much adore.

Nothing derails me from my goal
So I press on, daring and bold,
All through the days and through the nights
With all my strength I hold on tight.

To me it favors do or die.
I'll move the earth and then the sky
To reach my precious carrot stick
So far yet so close to my beak.

Like an ass led with carrot stick,
Though I remain quiet and meek
I burn in the yearn for your love
And so I pray to God above.

For He alone give loving treats
To praying souls as He sees fit.
Though to the world it seems futile
I pray and wait in the meanwhile.

Like a toddle craving cookie
That way upon the shelf he'd see,
Relentlessly kisses and pouts
And overwhelms dad with no doubt

I beg and beg, then beg some more
For your heart I yearn so much for.
Since good things, be it soon or late
Nudge always those who pray and wait.

My Darling

Just wanted to tell you how sweet your embrace feels
And how holding you near marvels me to the chills.
The magic of the bay, the still peace of your room
Made that last Sunday night ecstatic, free of gloom.

I had to be away from what I so treasure
To swear not to ever refrain from such pleasure.
You made me feel so new, so warm and so alive
That I declare aloud that you're my better halve.

I love you my darling and for so strong reasons
That I often wonder why do I stay alone.
But to rush is to fail. Nothing is finalized
Unless it is over and over analyzed.

So darling we'll get there though again we may face
Either tougher rival or even bigger mace.
Enough, I said enough, let me just end my rhyme
With the sweet taste I have of getting back my prime.

My Wife

I prayed and prayed
For a beautiful wife
To cast away
The sadness of my life

Just when I thought
My dream would not come true,
Sad and distraught
I looked up; there were you.

So here I am, I come to you,
My soul on its knees, comes anew,
Begging like a child in distress
For its due share of happiness.

To You # 1

I stand before you, knocking at your door,
I stand before you as I did before.
I stand before you, all naked and poor
With only my love sung as an encore.

Repeatedly I hear: "Go your own way,
I'm living my life, find yours in the hay.
You left it down there, acting so foolish,
Be a man for once, it's over, finished."

But here I still stand like a lonely dog
All afraid to go and face the thick fog.
I have one mistress, a lovely lady,
How can I ever exist or be me
If she doesn't hold secure of my leash;
I'd surely one day, get lost and perish.

O darling I beg, listen to my plea,
It's again the voice of your poor baby
Coming back to life from his misery
And praying out loud for you to marry.

You know if ever I had another,
Never but never would they make waver
This heart beating strong but for you only
Which if in your hands would be so merry.

Honey I just can't forget about you.
God knows how I tried, tried to start anew
But always your face, so sweet in my hands,
Eclipse all others who between us stand.
I will forever beg for your pardon
And don't ask me why and for what reason
You should to my plea give your attention.
I'd gladly reply – no hesitation –
Listen to your heart for there still resides
The love of me you so hard tried to hide.

I often picture this blessed evening
When my eyes on you will do a landing.
The stars in the sky will surely rejoice
And in their own way will second your choice.

This world will remain a sorrowful place,
It will rain sometimes, the moon won't change face.
The sun will always warm us with its rays
But even among this known disarray

I know with your love, the world will be kind
For the sole reason that you're on my mind.
If only you knew how much I cherish
The fall when it puts on leaves its finish.
This just reminds me of you my baby,
See how much I learnt from you, my Junie.

I'll try not to bore you any longer
Though I spilled my guts unlike no other
I hope that within your heart you still have
The strength you once had to show me the path
Back into your arms. For there I desire
Comes rain or comes shine to live the entire
Rest of this ordeal that you call my life
Hoping that safe there, I'll settle my strife.

I stand before you, knocking at your door,
I stand before you like never before.
I stand before you with my heart still sore.
I stand before you hear my poor downpour.

The Memories Of You

Suddenly in a most insidious manner,
Invading my deep soul, drowning every fiber,
Leaving powerless, weak, almost on my knees
This strong hold that I prayed for the Lord to release,
Just when I think my life finally springs anew,
Reach the shores of my mind the memories of you.

Oh how can I describe the divine hours spent,
That deep inside my heart would almost make me faint.
We were only touching one another's fingers,
Breaking thee orient ice of those years of silver…
I loved you so dearly, but what else could I do?
Never thought I would have the memories of you.

They hurt like hunger pain on an empty stomach.
Like painful needle sticks they stop you on your track.
They invade your psyche; go straight up to your id,
Run up and down your mind not ever losing speed.
They torture, lacerate…As if they were taboo,
Never would I've traded the memories of you.

They may not make me feel of your hands the caress,
They may not stand by me when I am in distress.
They may not sound as sweet and lovely as you do
Or even just stay there waiting to say, "I do"
But until you enter into my life anew
I will always treasure the memories of you.

Brand-New

The lovely shade of pink and blue,
Reminder of love pure and true,
Cuts through the hearts of me and you,
Setting for us a brand-new stage.

These true colors never hand-made
And of scenes thus far never played,
That make all other colors fade,
Keeping us daily in His cage.

We never knew when it began
But gladly we followed the band,
Saddling safely the wagon stand
Leading us surely to the bliss.

All in life is bestowed for sure.
What befell us is blessing pure,
Souls to mercifully allure;
Tangible proof of His promise.

Soothed by His embrace we marvel
For on this journey we travel,
All stories slowly unravel
To gladly make all dreams come true.

My Future Wife

You must be somewhere waking up
Or this day about to wrap up.
Your parents around you may be
Caring for you every hobby.

Or is it that alone like me
You're moping in your misery?
Are you somewhere soaking the sun
Or in a place where rays there' none?

Does it matter? Not so ever.
For you, my heart in its whispers,
Rehearses over and over
The words of love that it harbors.

We'll meet one day or have we yet
Exchanged words that we did forget?
Does it matter, does it ever?
Love's always been a pathfinder.

Ode To Marijune

Just like the sun upon my sphere,
The thoughts of you come bright and clear
And they bud in the depths of me
A crave for your hand, my Junie.

Never in my life has it been,
Never, repeatedly I screened,
Never has it been that I long
For any living soul that long.

My morning sun seems weak and dull,
The moonlight my dreams, just can't lull,
The seasons come and bring new songs
But you air rings ever so strong.

Many mornings my tears I brunch,
But my pillow they always drench
Cannot echo your lovely voice
When your dear name becomes sweet noise.

The Sore Thumb

The sore thumb stands alone,
No one to its rescue.
When the damage is done
It's always black and blue.

The sore thumb never tells
Its half of the story.
You never hear the bells,
No query, no jury.

The sore thumb will attempt
To pick up the pieces.
It just hides the contempt
Felt by all the misses.

The sore thumb, au contraire,
Tries so hard to restore
Any blow, any tear,
And that's a metaphor.

The sore thumb will one day
Fix itself safe and sound,
For the soul come what may
Of the Spirit abounds.

The sore thumb will join then
The faraway siblings,
The ones called his brethren
And His praises will sing.

Never, never again
Will it stand all alone.
No more sore, no more pain,
Just a call on the phone.

Nowatimes

The brisk autumnal wind blowing
Over the meadows of your mind
Failed to rekindle the cuddling
Of yesterdays you left behind.

So tenderly you hold her hand,
Regurgitating tender thoughts
But sadly what she couldn't stand
Landed despite how hard she fought.

So you remained in her embrace
Hoping it'd be temporary
But the grimace upon her face
Revealed it was in no hurry.

But in the meanwhile of your eve
Where time erupts at lightning speed
Your heart explodes right on your sleeve
But leaves her lenity arid…

Nowatimes, a few years ago,
Each and every time autumn lands
The subtlety of her sorrow
Rests heavy on her harshness stand.

So peacefully, like summer brook,
You regain your seat of candor
Qualming softly the time it took
To regain your youthful ardor.

My Infused Love

I come humbly to let you know
How my whole life belongs to you.
All through my highs, all through my lows,
Despite my fog, your light shines through.

I come humbly when time's at hand
To pour my whole self at your feet.
All that I made, all that I planned
Breathe your body, mind and spirit.

I come humbly and don't pretend
To be the one sharing your dreams.
But rather I want to attend
At the least of your silent screams.

So on my knees I come humbly
Daily to count you my worries.
Funny how jovial and bubbly
My spirit flips in a hurry.

For to your almost divine grace
I'll always bring my weary soul
And to you and your lovely face
Forever give my heart to hold.

And naturally when times are rough
And my spirit travels wobbly,
When all dopey I reach my trough,
Again to you I'll come humbly.

Sweet Apology

I brought you roses, though perishable,
They are to many the most palpable
Of love expression.
I brought you roses, although standing here,
I don't really know if you want to hear
Of my confusion.

I'd say I love you, but of this you're sure
And though you respond with feelings so pure
I know that you doubt of our tomorrow;
You were hurt again, still fresh your sorrow.

If the Lord above decides to ignore
Or fails to bless us, for which I implore,
We will forever quarrel then depart
Then after a while seek each other's heart…

Let us in pure wisdom be with one another
And give the final word to the Lord, our Savior.

The Month Of Angels

When nature finally unravels her beauty
For so long kept unsung, for so long kept in sheaves,
When the sun seems to be so daring and haughty
And every living thing regains the will to live,

When the flowers again open up lovingly
To offer all the birds sample so hard to choose,
From fragrance, shapes and shades presented randomly,
Bewildered eyes to see and troubled souls to soothe,

That's when I think of you, for from my horizon,
The spirit in the air brings me the scent of you.
The month of May begets the best of the season
And sets a lovely stage for love to spring anew.

The month of all mothers remains the mother month
Which seems to be the door of all nature treasures.
The month of all mothers, always from its mere trough,
Daily brings up the world to summertime pleasures.

Always mother knows best so from rain come flowers.
And with the sun warming the birds sing cheery tunes.
But the best gift of all, free from scattered showers,
Of mother month of May comes precious month of June.

For long, so long ago, before the dawn of time,
They carefully ponder over your month of birth.
It was among it all; warm sun, flowers, bird chimes
That it was decided to send you here on Earth.

So when the month of May comes with all its fanfare
And when nature adorns her precious apparel,
They tell the universe tenderly to prepare
For peaceful month of June, famous month of angels.

Tweedy Bird

O my Tweedy of love, my little bird of love,
Will you one day decide to nest in my alcove?
Night and day, day and night, I sit at my window.
I see sun, I see rain, I even bear the snow
But none seems to carry the echo of your wings.
Come with your jolly tune and teach my heart to sing.

O my Tweedy of love, the little bird I love,
Will you one of these days drop from the sky above?
Long ago it has been since I last saw the glow,
The glow of your brown eyes, so placid and mellow.
The years have come and gone and yet they failed to bring
Some solace to my soul, an end to my starving.

Hurry

Hurry and give your life to me,
Hurry, my dear, time is at hand.
Hurry before spring leaves the land
And slides into dichotomy.

Hurry and give your life to me,
Come give me my fulfilling dose
For if the petals yield the rose
Surely our days will be balmy.

Hurry and give your life to me
For if ever angels are sent
To straighten was has been so bent,
They'd have your lovely eyes Mammy.

Hurry and give your life to me
Then in the stillness of the nights
We'll set our world of stars aright,
Right on the lake of Dulcamy.

My Marijune

To the heck of the girl I love,
The one I can't get enough of,
I want to send this written kiss
Just so she knows how much she's missed.

I quiver, quiver all inside,
Though many times I tried to hide
The effect her lovely brown eyes
Provoke in me they hypnotize.

My hands are still seeking the touch
Of her hands, her skin and so much.
Always she's the one to instill
Within my soul her warmth so real.

So to this little girl I love,
This precious, petable, sweet dove
I offer a whole world of these,
Kisses and hugs…what a délice!

To You Again

To this love given to my life,
This precious chosen companion,
Silent escort on this long path
Leading me right back to Zion,

To the God sent little angel,
Bearing His love upon her wings,
Willing so kindly to travel
The length of miles thus remaining,

To the joyful dove hovering
Over the dullness of my soul,
Promising so many treasure
And so willing to pay my toll

To this rare pearl finally found
To finalize my diadem
Who brought me of Heaven the sound
Within her voice that always tames

Whatever drives deep within me,
I give my heart, mind, and body,
And though the world may disagree
I give my soul complete and free.

The Realm Of Love

O my meadow with golden springs,
My violin with supple strings,
The melody that my heart sings,
My docile waves of lonely sea.

How sweet becomes the lullaby
Whispered as though it were a sigh,
Surging from lips that do not lie
To dip your world in ecstasy.

To love so deep, to love so strong
That you ignore the tearing prongs
To rid from your life all that's wrong
And restore your sweet infancy.

Even torture would not disclose
This candor to any of those
Who begged to differ so they chose
To just disregard what they see.

So calling to the better half:
Time for us to follow the path
And like the cow and the sweet calf
Take heed though there's no urgency.

For deeply the snares penetrate,
Deeply they come to permeate
The soul the heart slowly dictates,
To brand the mind with no mercy.

My Love, will you ever fathom
Whether you're Eve and he's Adam,
Love will conquer every atom
Of hearts as blessed prophecy.

Therefore my sweet child, take courage,
Give into this divine bondage,
And of love choose to be hostage,
There, I dispel the secrecy.

No one can size the realm of love
Given to us from God above.

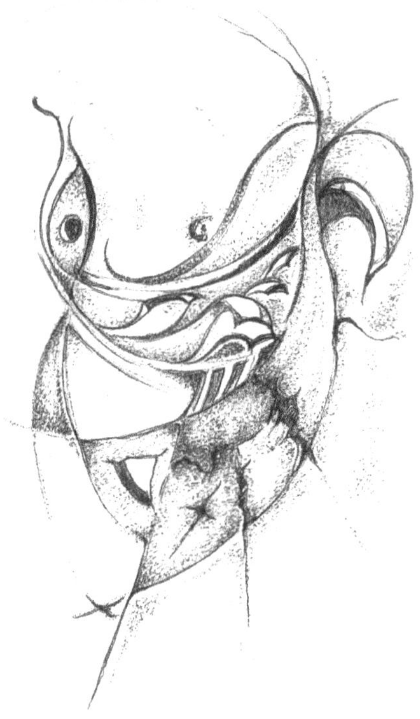

When My Junie Was Mine

I don't know why I try to write thoughts of this kind.
Maybe cause day and night they occupy my mind
Or maybe just because the mere fact of writing
Open large avenues for deeper soul searching.

Every time I awake my faithful memory,
I marvel at the point I reach; sad and teary.
It brings about a flow of strong and gushing blood,
It brings about the time when on my turf she trod.

Yes when Junie was mine I never had a clue,
Looking at that young girl, that my dream had come true.
I gambled night and day, betting on her strong love,
Disregarding the signs, sheer warnings from above.

Each time I went away I could not fathom why
That sense of doom I felt would bring me heavy sighs.
But the fool that I was never saw the cold tomb
Awaiting my poor self, lined up with finest gloom.

So when Junie was mine slowly I let her go,
So much desiring to restart from zero.
But little did I know that when she left the nest
My cold and stifling soul followed the very best.

Your Face

I often consider from the depths of my heart
The reasons why I melt, losing all assurance,
Find it hard to focus, like having an infarct,
Fighting for every word, almost like in a trance.

Yet this inner snafu, this internal chaos
Causing my heart to gear, racing the Daytona,
Provokes in my psyche a strong surge of pathos,
Leaving me weak, faintly, just like a madonna.

This mother of feeling of my throat grabs a hold
And the knot I swallow seems to have many peers
And the smile I expose seems to favor pure gold
For it comes underline my many inner fears.

And I feel I could kneel; I'd be so much closer
To the ground that I feel I might hit anytime.
Since it is the posture adequate for prayer,
I pray hoping my voice rings not like a fake chime.

Painfully I attempt to show some composure.
I had always excelled at keeping it inside
And slowly deliver, carefully, with measure,
This gush of affection, the love I cannot hide.

But deep within my eyes I know it can be seen,
The lovely, jolly cause of my discountenance.
Come and look into them and enjoy the whole scene;
Your pretty face my dear, of divine countenance.

How Sweet It Is

The tree repeatedly comes knock at the window,
The sky connivingly winks at us here below.
Butterflies frantically come in and out of sight,
A lizard in the wind holds to the rock so tight.
In this land so stingy, with no mall, no theater,
We are truly lucky to have one another
But the old waterfall breaks the code of silence
Reminding seemingly to us its existence.

Your hand of mighty queen holding a cigarette
Unknowingly ordains honor, love and respect.
And I the horny pig, calling your attention,
Pining for your sweet lips, your thighs; my devotion.
But in this rainy land, where sunny days are poor,
Day after day we learn to love us more and more.
From one wood to others, in this vibrant forest,
I invite you my love, come and give me your best.

My Promise

One day if the good Lord allows,
One day of fall, to say the least,
One day I'll gladly take my vows,
One day I'll do what I promised.

The morning rain would have just stopped,
The sun would then shine a bit pale,
The birds from their nests would come pop;
They'd all rush to witness the tale.

Nature tends, in a lot of ways,
To prepare special happenings.
Even the earth won't speed away
From the bliss this good day will bring.

One day therefore, of clear blue sky,
One day, strolling along the pier,
With witnesses, the passers-by,
I'll entrust to you my life, dear.

One Day

One of these days will spring, one of these blesséd days,
One special day made of pure laughter on the rocks.
Of day of mid-autumn, of untangled dreadlocks,
One day of sheer blossom, of essence of Olay.

One day that stands alone and carries its burden,
One day of pure thin air and low humidity.
One day with saddle fine and solid unity,
One day of gardenias over a toddle's den.

One blesséd blue-sky day with bed of scented rose,
One day of Christmas Eve with magi in limo.
One precious day of days with more highs than of lows,
One day inspiring all the rhymes and the prose.

One day that would render other days pitiful,
One day that'd make amend for futuristic faults.
One day just like the day that'd open heaven's vault
And put you in my arms, free, loving and peaceful.

When I Think Of You

Early in the morning when I first realize
That my milieu my heart, just ceased to mesmerize,
When I have to emerge from this bundle of sheets
Lacking the zest to thrive my dejected spirit,
When even the sunshine, or the clouds or the rain,
The birds or the squirrel, the early morning train
Seem to be worth a pence; that's when I think of you.

When faced with the cold fact that I will have again
To mingle with the crowd, my daily bread to gain,
When the food I ingest just cannot seem to please
My palate too blazé from many brands of cheese,
When even all my faith in the good Lord above
Just cannot alleviate the grief I tried to shove,
When nothing else matters; that's when I think of you.

See, the Master of love teaches us to follow
Our hearts where He speaks, where His Spirit echoes,
But I hope He offers, as an all-divine grace,
To my despairing heart His almighty solace
For without His favor, without His compassion
The mere fact of being merges to depression…
But if my plea He shuns, right there I think of you.

When the shadow settles and darkness embraces
The day overburdened from the chores and races,
When all is said and done and promises are few,
When the care spread around returns to molest you,
When the birds, the squirrels, and the clouds and the rain
Seem unable to sing to me any refrain;
When nothing else will do, again I think of you.

My Swallow

My swallow has landed
Despite her broken wings.
She flew but went stranded,
Laden with sufferings.

My swallow has landed,
She dropped down in her nest.
She came empty handed
But with love in her chest.

My swallow has landed
Despite her many tears.
Her heart of love loaded
Made it easy to steer.

And so with arms opened,
Ready to love I stand
For now until the end
My swallow is on land.

Listen...

I could tell you one day
How empty and senseless
Life can be without you.
I could tell you to stay
For my world becomes less
Dreary, my sky turns blue...
But to tell you all this
Would you ever believe,
Take it in or dismiss?

I could show you one day
How quickly I regress
To nothing until you
With your angelic way
And your kisses that bless
Come and give me brand new
Hope and strength that I miss
Cause from you I receive
My sorrow and my bliss.

Many more than one way
Lead to sheer happiness
But they hurt through and through.
This love that you display
With genuine gentleness
Springs life in me anew
So thank God for all this,
This treasure I retrieve,
Like a sacred chalice.

Your Name

At the sound of your name
My heart is set aflame.
It keeps me all febrile,
Shaken for a long while,
Emotionally drained,
Of your stamp deeply stained.

I can almost palpate
My deep fidgety state.
This overwhelming blush
Is my blood in a gush
Demanding that I quell
This rush I know so well.

At the sound of your name
I feel mellow and tamed,
All my strength set apart
Just to sustain my heart
Throbbing in euphoria,
Wrapped within your aura.

I can hear it often,
I hear it mostly when,
Left alone with my mind,
It is you I run find.
There, weary, quite loony,
I can meet my Junie.

My True Love

The inspiration arising
From deep within the hushed up soul
Comes all stamped up, loudly crying,
Unveiling to us stirring tolls.

There, in the midst of black and white
We read clearly the promises
So unspoken and out of sight
Though their words bear hugs and kisses.

It's always an opened window
Of lonely cage left in the cold.
From it will escape a swallow,
First sign of what is yet untold.

So when my pen speeds unafraid,
Revealing thoughts branded by you,
With no scheme, ponder what is said;
I brag of you, my love so true.

The Right Time

The right time never fails,
The right time never trails.
It's always so punctual
To display the usual
Load of kronos power
To tackle whatever
Befalls a certain one
Whose task is still undone.

The right time never tries
To provoke the demise
Of the time it follows.
It is always too close
To the time that is born
Right after. But it scorns
The futuristic plans
That are built up in vain.

The right time will always
Question the dragging ways
We delay the action
Under its dominion.
So it kindly reminds
The aftermath that hinds
Frank procrastination
And begets deception.

The right time will provoke
With repeated strokes
The waking of the will
Power of genuine steel.
For only a solid,
Determined, intrepid
Can profit of its span
And concretize the gain.

The right time won't perish.
It conveys what's cherished
To the moment in line,
With a similar spine
Well able to carry
The task that's in query.
It tries to dissipate
The scent of being late.

The right time will prevail
And set us on the trail
Of desired success,
Displaying our prowess.
The right time of our love
Will come straight from above
To kiss the bleeding hearts
That it once set apart.

Since No One Else Will Do

Since no one else will do
Like a soldier I stand
Wounded, with loaded hands
Of dreams that didn't come true.

Since no one else will do
I'll re-shoulder the load
Of hopes and dreams of old
Starring me, starring you.

Since no one else will do
I'll focus on yearning
And praying and hoping
For your heart to take you

To me the sole one who,
For some twenty-five years
And so, so many tears,
Misses you, you, my Boo.

The rest of my life through,
Since there's me, since there's you,
I'll stand waiting for you;
Since no one else will do.

To You # 2

Do you know how much I love you?
Can you fathom how truly blue
My sky becomes, the so rare times
Your thoughts with mine decide to rhyme?

Just so you know, just so you know,
I'll seek your love through high and low.
But if you want that I remain
At your feet, gladly I'll domain.

My Words

Sometimes the words that I shower
Your ears, as a passionate kiss,
Are never robed in the power
I try to share with you I miss.

They remain lame, they remain weak,
They fail miserably too much.
They don't carry the warmth I seek,
To melt you heart with hugs and such.

But repeatedly they emerge
Trying to bring my loving stamp
And more than often what they surge
Is an image all pale and damp.

But they come back with the intent
To reach their goal next time around.
And they won't feel any content
Until from them pure love abound.

And so my words relentlessly
Will come caress your lovely ears
Till they dislodge successfully
From within you all trace of fear.

Your Brown Eyes

Lakes of the bluest waves
Reflect the sky above
And the clouds come and pave
A steady trail of love
Never before heard of.

And the sunny meadow
Saddled by month of May
Seem to give the rainbow
A colorful array
As show of a fair play.

But when I see your eyes
At each glorious dawn
My soul is mesmerized
As ingenuous fawn
Caught in the fairest lawn.

Come whisper to my ears
Still in lunar slumber
Then the stampede that starts,
Sets fire bright amber
On walls of my chamber.

Your eyes, in the exile
Land where I don't reside
Set the mood on the isles
To rekindle the tide
Where my destiny hides.

Your eyes take for a spin
My soul and make it grow
Come the thick or the thin
Into a lovely glow
Of winter's purest snow.

My Dusk

When the sun takes a bow
Deep within the June sky
It hints me that for now
It's time to freely sigh
And this way, decompress
And let precious matters,
Like the ones that obsess,
Rise to the gray matter.

Right there the dusk falling
Laden with its shadows
Seems to erase all things
The day had to borrow.
And so it makes a trail
Sown up of dust of stars,
Bright as a comet tail,
Visible from afar.

It heralds the peaceful
Feeling of end of day.
It precedes the painful
Void that in me you laid.
For nothing in this world,
Under this dark blue sky,
Can stead you, little girl,
Nothing even comes shy.

The falling dusk brings then
Amongst its precious stars
The trail of you, dear friend,
As I exit the car.
It is the sole highlight
Sought for all through the day.
It makes my eve so bright,
My end of day so gay,

Ode To My Junie

Never will you unfold this puzzling mystery
That daily I sustain deep in my heart and mind,
Never, I say never, do not waste your query;
The cause remains hidden, not for the world to find.

The mighty waves of sea cover lesser treasure,
Even the universe offers no such richness.
And the immense azure so blue in its rapture
Still retells but poorly the charms of my mistress.

From the dawn of the day till the sun retires,
From the East to the West, even between the Poles,
From the driest of sands, right where the sun fires
To the greenest pasture with merry bunny holes,

Nothing offers a sound warmer in decibels,
Nothing can bring a tune with better harmony,
Nothing, I say nothing; the universe babbles
When it nears the warm voice of my lovely Junie.

God's Love

The time we spend searching for love
Should be spent with the God above
For only He knows well our hearts.

He provides for our every need
And He daily all spirits feeds
For He made us all from the start.

He came on earth to spread His Love,
The love we are so in need of,
The one that makes us wise and smart.

For only by sharing His love
In return we get from above
The fondest desires of our hearts

Sunday Without You

So from the early dawn still peering through the fog
I could perceive myself sleeping like a big log.
Since I barely could move from this, my somnolence
I left my alert mind recapture your absence.

Right there, my heart startled and strongly skipped a beat
Refusing to behave far away from its treat.
It will have once again to show some bravado
And go through one more day without your heart's echo.

Painfully I stretched out just reaching for the phone
To see if a message made through silent tone.
Nothing. Nothing from you. Nothing. What an abyss!
How can I catch my breath with your voice that I miss?

But today is Sunday; it should not be a drag;
Any feeling of blues should be put in a bag.
But the air without you is heavy on the chest;
Of all its elements, it lacks the very best.

So the sun finally made it through the thick clouds.
Though it shined at its best it failed to melt the shroud
Hanging around my soul. So I went on my way
Trying to breathe my best without you this Sunday.

On My Mind

The thoughts of you that linger on
Give me rainbow to glide upon.
They mastermind a safe heaven
Where I retire quite often.

There, all my dreams of me and you
Never leave my elated view.
They free my soul of all bondage
And to my heart they give courage.

Never knowing a dull moment,
Always giving me great content.
They can, if given direction,
Cause a spectrum of emotions.

For if ever you were to shun
My plea for some rays of your sun,
These thoughts of bliss and revelry
Would turn to hell and misery.

For my world's so wrapped around you;
It can be bright, it can be blue.
It can be built or fall apart
All based on the mood of your heart.

So when you come and nudge my soul
Keep in mind that you take control
Of this fellow so far away
Who bear your thoughts in bare display.

Nightcall

How tender is the night,
One night of early fall!
Soft and sultry recall
Of childhood mem'ries bright.

How gentle is the night,
One night of subtle breeze
With mind and soul at ease
Holding on to love tight!

How lovely is the night
With silent symphonies,
Old love affair queries
And painful wish-I-might's!

Lo! The gentlest of nights
Brings to me, brings to all
The long forgotten calls
Of soulmate out of sight.

Your Coming

One day just like today
One day with no display
One day of sun or rain
One day of joy or pain
One day after a day
Following a Thursday
Or maybe a Sunday;
It's such a blessed day.
But it'll be a good day
For you'll be on your way
To me who, as they say,
From June to month of May
Wait for you, my chérie.
So on this day, I say,
Call me Sean, call me Ray
Or call blessed too,
I'll look up and see you…
And so right then and there
I will know that somewhere,
Maybe deep in the hearts,
There's a God who imparts
Graces to His children
When He sees them in pain…
It will be a good day,
The one that gently sways
Your lovely steps to me.

Stress-Free

One of these days I'll look at you
And see the girl for whom I yearn.
One of these days, gray or clear blue,
Your lovely face I will discern.

The painful bridge you're now crossing
Requires of you a stiff toll.
You're taking it but your sighing
Attests your strife; mind against soul.

It's never the end of the world;
This I want you to remember.
Life takes its course and will unfurl
Whether you're awake or slumber.

What is written will come to be
Despite all attempts to hold on.
So let go and let God and see
The bright sun at your horizon.

I wish you the best in your life,
This never-ending give and take.
If of turmoil it is so rife
It's to best teach you what's at stake.

You live and learn, so do the same,
Soon your troubles will be all gone.
Don't lose hope and call on His Name
Thus far He has failed to help none.

One of these day I'll see my boo,
As beautiful as she can be.
One of these days I'll come to you
When you're dilemmas will all flee.

Heartfelt Prayer

Now that Flushing, New York, with its overcast dome,
Its ever-busy streets, loaded buses and cars,
Its cold and snowy days, no more are called my home,
I can grasp what nature offers to me so far.

Now that all that I lost is for ever made clear,
Duped, coerced and mislead,
Now that I realized the treasure held so dear
By the void left instead,

Now that on this seashore, so warm and so friendly,
All touched by the eerie crimson evening display,
I can finally scope and perceive vividly
The trickery performed, sheer cause of my dismay,

Now that nothing hinders the flow of souvenirs,
Of missing her brown eyes,
Now that, O my dear Lord, who remains always near
To those many despise,

Now that all that I see of goodness, warmth and sun,
Loudly seem to confess Your deep Love for Your brood,
The tears that now I shed atone, sine qua non
For having so bluntly disregarded the good

That You bestow on us, proof of Your loving care.
Your wisdom surpasses
And though your ways are just, no one should ever dare
Waste Your given graces.

So belovéd Father, You handed me a rose
And in my troubled mind I left her all alone.
Now every ounce of tears she sheds in her repose
Will be taken to me, for my soul to atone.

You know, blessed Father, how precious are the tears
Shed by Your innocents.
And never an instant, fail You ever to hear
Their pleas when they are sent.

You see deep in the hearts every hidden motive,
You see the contrition that ravages the soul.
You see, and it's for us a blessed incentive,
To hope for Your goodness to again make us whole.

For the angels summoned to evolve among us,
Not all have the same clout.
We only recognize the size of their genius
When they leave with sad pout.

We so poorly perceive only one side of facts.
The true meaning exists safely in Your domain.
Lovingly You take us along the chosen tract
Although, to heed Your voice, so stubborn we remain.

My uttered contrition and sought for forgiveness
To Your mercy, appeal.
Send her again my way, so that through Your goodness
My embrace she could feel.

My Dear One

You, the one I long for,
Long deep within the core,
Can you feel its fierce pace
Missing your sweet embrace?

It throbs as to rejoice
At the sound of your voice,
Then ends in a flutter
When you leave thereafter.

I try so hard to quell
Its all-quivering spell
But the sound of your name
Makes it react the same.

This lovely sounding name
Within me, gives all fame
To my heart steady croon
Calling you, Marijune

So every word you say
Carries my mind away
And every thought that may
Pulsates my mind astray.

But for so many times
It answered to love chimes;
Some lovely you could tell,
Others sounded like knell.

But for you my jolie
It wakes up suddenly;
Like the sun on my night,
You dissipate my fright.

You I long to embrace
But does not feel the pace
Of the beat of my heart,
Will you tear it apart?

What Took You So Long

What took you so long little dove?
I waited for you for so long
I waited, writing down this song
Just to reveal to you my love.

What took you so long lovely dove?
I waited for you day and night,
Burning steadily candlelight
That could lead you to my alcove.

I waited drowning in my tears,
Curled up under this inner fear
That I would never see you again,
With heart throbbing at each sunrise,
Expecting I would get my prize
And see my queen her throne, regain.
What took you so long my sweet dove?
I waited for you for so long,
Enduring every single prong
That your absence in my heart shoved

What took you so long little dove?
I waited through the falling rain
That steadily watered my pain
Although the sun shone from above.

I waited for you hopelessly,
Wishing that you would hear my plea,
Bring back my tweedy bird to me.
And this desert seems so dreary
That a lonely soul gets weary
As he drags his awful infamy.

What took you so long my sweet dove?
I waited for you much too long,
I waited for you with heart strong,
Jumping each time you were thought of

I waited for you and you came
Like thunder in a clear blue sky,
You came and choke down every sigh.
My life will never be the same;
From now on.... You're here!!!